"In Your LIFETIME, Follow The LIGHT, Not The DARKNESS"

M. PETERSEN

To Norma Jean - My soul - sister In Christ Jesus

Michelle Petersen
3/30/2015

Order this book online at www.trafford.com
or email orders@trafford.com

Most Trafford titles are also available at major online book retailers.

Printed in the United States of America.

ISBN: 978-1-4669-8035-8 (sc)
ISBN: 978-1-4669-8037-2 (hc)
ISBN: 978-1-4669-8036-5 (e)

Library of Congress Control Number: 2013902616

Trafford rev. 11/09/2013

 www.trafford.com

North America & international
toll-free: 1 888 232 4444 (USA & Canada)
fax: 812 355 4082

DEDICATION

I dedicate this book to my children and future grandchildren. I hope that my words of wisdom will help them on their own life's journey towards the Light of God's Love.

I also dedicate this book to all the spiritual seekers who are looking for answers as they walk life's journey on our Beloved Mother Earth.

CONTENTS

LIFE IS AN INITIATION . . . .

. . . . of life's lessons, and of life's testing's, to see what our soul is made of. The choices we make whether that of light or darkness, whether we choose this pathway or that pathway, will fashion the remainder of our lives. Think about it and CHOOSE WELL. We are in the school of learning called earth. Our inner soul has chosen to link with the physical body of humanity. Think about your life down the road, maybe, twenty, thirty, or maybe by the age of forty. I am now in my fifty's and still working on the next phase of my life. Think about what it would take to accomplish this goal you have made for yourself and pave out a plan to make it happen. Where do your interests take you? What is in your heart's desire if you could do anything you wanted to do? Ask the creator spirit of your soul for help along the way. What we picture in our mind's eye can transpire in due time if we keep focused on our goals. Its okay to let those goals expand or change as we live out our life. If we listen to our heart, it will lead us in the right direction in the course of our life, keeping in mind not to cause any harm to ourselves and others. The age old saying: "Treat others the way that you would like to be treated", is an eternal truth. Listen to the promptings of your mind and inner guidance system. Invite the light of the mother-father God's love . . . . fill your heart, body, mind, and soul.

So, my question to you is this . . . .

What are your choices in the course of your own life? Do you choose the "light" of the matter; that which is good and wholesome, or do you choose the darker path, driven by ego's lower animal instincts of self-gratification, what I personally refer to the dragon within.

REMEMBER THAT EVERY DAY IS A FRESH NEW START . . . .

Each day we are faced with a new beginning. Take one step at a time, one day at a time, one week, one month, and one year at a time. Let time unfold before your eyes like the petals of a flower opening up to its full potential. Each day arises with a clean slate. We have another chance to make things right with the world if needed.

SIGNIFICANCE VERSUS INSIGNIFICANCE . . . .

I often feel quite insignificant as I walk on the face of our Mother Earth. I feel like one small voice in the sea of many voices. How could my own small voice drown out the others or speak out loud enough to make a significant change for the betterment of the whole populous. I'm just one small insignificant person. But I say different now that I have walked the earth for almost sixty years now. Our lives touch so many others over the course of a life time. A simple smile to a stranger or a kind word of encouragement can make all the difference in someone else's day. You have heard of the wise parable of a stone being thrown into a pool of still water. The stone soon sinks to the bottom of the watery pool, but the force of the stone pushes the surrounding water to form circles of waves in all directions at once. This force of nature can be used to describe our own actions for they too put out an energy force that touches the lives of those around us. We can choose whether that force is of the light to be a creation of love and joy for our fellow man, or that of darkness that has the same energy flow, but rather immerses those around them with the karmic effects of wrong doing; creating betrayal, greed, hate, selfishness and discord to name a few.

IT'S NEVER TOO LATE
TO CHANGE . . . .

BECOME one of the SONS/DAUGHTERS OF LIGHT versus one of the sons/daughters of darkness. Choosing the path of light and love during your lifetime is a choice of goodness in a kind and humble way; not haughty or self-righteous, but that of politeness and respectful communication. We have to admit that there is goodness and evil in this world of duality. Within the anatomy of our inner soul, in the center of our etheric heart's core, holds a portion of energy from the source of creation.

There is an aperture somewhat like that of a camera lens that opens or closes in this center chamber of the heart of our soul. When we think or feel positive thoughts of goodness towards ourselves or to our fellow man, our heart's center opens up and is filled with the essence of positive energy, love, and light. When we focus on negative thoughts our heart's center closes and we can feel the darkness within; our heart burns with a discomfort of darkness, so we learn from our mistakes and we can choose again. We can make better choices with each new moment and each new day. Ask the spirit of God to open your heart to the alchemy and emotion of God's love.

BAD DAYS COME AND GO . . . .

This too will pass in time. Time heals everything sooner or later. Don't give up on your life. Pray for the right answers. Contemplate or meditate on what is the best thing to do, even if it is to walk away or ignore the problem for a while. You will know when to act in a kind hearted way, or when it is time to set boundaries to keep your own life sacred and productive. Choose the right circle of friends that keep your life healthy. I have been thrown a few curve balls throughout my journey. While it may take some time to digest what has happened, we can only move forward from there. Sometimes it takes many years to iron out the mishaps. Eventually, time will take its course; healing will take place if you allow it. When I don't know what to do, I have found that the best thing is to ask for help and guidance in prayer. Asking God to help carry my burdens; solutions transpire in due time.

SURVIVE THE DARK NIGHT OF THE SOUL . . . .

There will be challenging times in the seasons of our soul's journey. Be patient with yourself. When life seems so dark at times, don't give up; ride it out to the end of the storm. I promise you, this too will pass. The darkness of the storm will eventually subside. The light of the sun will rise again. Ask God for help and for guidance. Ask for a proper solution to any given problem that might present itself in your lifetime. The answers may not crop up into your conscience mind immediately. But somehow the right person may cross your path with the right advice that you are looking for. You might read a book or hear something on the radio that is exactly what you need. You might be led to call someone on the phone to chat awhile. Whatever the answers will be that are provided for you, sometimes take time. Be patient. The real solution is to ASK GOD FOR HELP, and help will come in various ways.

WAIT FOR THE RAINBOW DAYS . . . .

When the storms of life pass, the rainbow days are worth waiting for, and believe me they will come. THE SUN ALWAYS RISES. Life has it's rewarding times too. We just have to wait and see what is around the bend in the road. The twists and turns in the course of life's journey can open up to the most beautiful moments and happy times too.

GOD REACHES OUT TO HIS/HER CHILDREN IN MANY WAYS . . . .

You cannot conceptualize God within the limits of scientific physicality; especially within the limited thinking of the Western world's train of thought. God does not play by the rules of limited human ignorance. Yes, there is a greater power within the heavens. This greater power is that of pure energy, immersed in love. The study of science will never be able to map out the etheric energy of God's pure consciousness, or contain it.

The world of spirit cannot be conceptualized by our ordinary physical senses. The etheric world of spirit is our true home. Our goal is to become one with this divine creation.

The stories in my book are true and valid beyond the measure of science. God is my witness. This book is not written for the viewpoint of a well-trained scholar, but from that of personal experience. The pages of my book are filled with a life time of experiential happenings. God often communicates to us through THOUGHT. He reaches out to each of us individually, in a personal way. We learn through experience. My journey is compiled of lessons of the soul.

FREE WILL . . . .

The earth is immersed within the plane of FREE WILL called duality. So this plane can either be that of blessing or curse, light or dark. Some days are likened to diamonds, others like stone.

The bible explains that as a man thinks . . . . so is he. Our lives are the result of our thoughts.

> (NKJV) Proverbs 23: Verse 7> "For as he thinks in his heart, so is he." . . . .

When we invite God into our lives in a PERSONAL way, He will do so if only we ask. However, GOD RESPECTS OUR FREE WILL; He does not force His thoughts or will upon you. If you don't invite the presence of Mother-Father God into your personal life's journey, then God seems distant.

If you turn your back on the truth of God's existence, then that will be your reality.

Our souls come to earth's life plane with the blessings of choice. We need only to ASK. Pray and God will listen. God forgives those who humble themselves, asking for guidance. Simply ask God to reveal himself to you in a personal way. Think with your heart, not with your five basic physical senses. Ask from the depth of your heart, that God will reveal himself to you in that of a spiritual nature, beyond the world of physicality. For the source of our soul's creation is from that of etheric pure energy of Light and Love. Blessings from God's out-reaching hand of enlightenment will not come your way unless you invite and ask for his intervention in your life. The choice is ours.

(NKJV) Colossians 3: Verse 2> "Set your mind on things above, not on things on the earth."

(NKJV) Psalm 37: Verse 3> "Trust in the Lord, and do good: Dwell in the land, and feed on His faithfulness. Verse 4> "Delight yourself also in the Lord, and He shall give you the desires of your heart. Verse 5> Commit your way to the Lord, Trust also in Him, and He shall bring it to pass. Verse 6> He shall bring forth your righteousness as the **light**, and your justice as the noonday.

> "IN YOUR LIFETIME, FOLLOW THE LIGHT, NOT THE DARKNESS".

These are the words spoken to me during my visionary near-death experience at the age of 15. I will tell you more as the pages of this book unfold.

LIFE HAS ITS CYCLES OF INITIATIONS . . . .

About every ten years, something profound would happen to me as I was growing up that was somewhat unexplainable in everyday terms. Looking back, it was like a predestined occurrence to test my character or to mold my soul into a new layer of awakening towards something that was a much higher power than mine self.

So here is my story from youth to adulthood; then beyond to middle age. I am still learning, still experiencing every day miracles with a life directed by the spirit of God. "Ask and you will receive", is a common saying amongst the spiritual teachings of old. Your life will be an amazing journey if you invite God to walk it with you. This doesn't mean that things will always turn out exactly like you may wish them to transpire, but it will surprise you in the end with just how wonderful life can be. Seek God's direction at every turn when you feel the need to do so. Spend time in quite prayer and contemplation. Listen to the inner promptings of your soul's journey. Answers and guidance will come to you like a download of information little by little. I have learned that the "greatest wisdom" is just an inner "knowing" > called "Gnosis" when written in Sanskrit.

A FRESH NEW BABY IN
A BASKET . . . .

My neighbor Harold use to tell me that he felt sorry for me as a three month old newborn baby, lying in a small basinet placed near several tall trees. My parents placed me there while they were building our cabin at the lake. It was strange to hear his words, "feeling sorry for you" because I have always loved these particular trees that he was referring to. They are located behind the house that was constructed so many years ago. To this day when I visit the lake home, I will at some point in my return, secretly slip back to these trees and look up at their tall branches. I then say in my own mind as in telepathic review, "I am home again". I have fond memories of the forest and the trees of this region. I grew up roaming the country side from the beaches on the lake to the top of the very large mountain behind our home. The view of the lake at the very pinnacle of the mountain is spectacular. It gives you an enhanced panoramic view of the entire lake which is about two miles in length and one mile in width. It's not unusual to see a bald eagle flying above or a deer roaming the country side. I was very fortunate to grow up in the company of this beautiful lake surrounded by several densely forested mountains. I refer to this lake as a "mountain lake" that still has its pristine beauty preserved by nature. Some of the lakes I see in the area where I now reside, I refer to as "city lakes" because they are surrounded by the skylines of many tall office buildings. Numerous homes are built on every inch surrounding the water front. When I was first born, this cabin home that was being built consisted of only one large rectangular room. Both of my parents worked and lived in the nearby town, so this was a secondary piece of land that they had purchased in the year of 1954. The price of which was eight hundred and fifty dollars with their hard earned money. They made monthly payments of fifty dollars until it was completely paid off. Our cabin had the usual kitchen, table, and living room. Towards the farthest corners of the room, it housed three bunk beds. My crib was carefully placed at one far left corner while the bunk beds lined up to the right of my space. They placed a very large curtain to separate the sleeping areas from the living room. The living room was graced with a very large picture window that overlooked the lake. My father had seen a nearby gas station in town that was being torn down. They had a sign that said "HELP YOURSELF" to any of the left over supplies lying on the ground. There was a very large window that was once part of the garage door of the old gas station's work area. He got the window for the right price, "free of charge" for just hauling it away! One of his brothers had a truck so this was an easy opportunity. In my younger years the cheapest wood was cedar so this was the wood of choice. The high peaked roof was surfaced with smooth aluminum roofing. Each winter, many feet of winter snow would slide right off of the cabin onto the front deck below. The wooden front deck was built around several tall trees that are still growing taller to this day. They shade the house quite well from the hot summer sun. Every few years the immediate space on the deck around the trees will need to be widened to permit room for growth. As you sit on the deck, the view of the lake is quite serene and peaceful. All in all it's like heaven on earth in this little remote country lake home.

We spent many weekends and summer vacations at the lake while I was growing up. I was able to learn how to swim like a fish from a very young age. My father and older brother found a business in town that allowed you to build your own speed boat if you paid for the supplies. So they made ends meet financially and soon after completed the boat! Now we had a speed boat to go water skiing and to take joy rides around the lake. I was in third grade when I first learned how to water ski. My feet were too small for the water skis so my brother had me leave on my tennis shoes to make a better fit. His patience finally paid off after about ten or twelve tries; I finally made it up on top of the water. It was incredible! I felt like I was flying for the very first time as my water skis glazed the surface of the water.

We also had our fishing boat. I remember eating a lot of freshly caught fish while growing up. On occasion we would motor boat to the narrows at the end of the lake that formed into the marsh lands. There, we would catch turtles with the fishing net. After taking them home we would place them into a wading pool and paint our initials on their backs with red fingernail polish. Eventually we would place them on the beach all lined up in a row and let them go. They would scatter off in all directions.

My dad was a very creative fisherman in his later years. The lake was teaming with what you call "mackinaws". These particular fish are bottom scavengers of this very deep lake. Because of this, they are very challenging to catch; they can age and grow to become a good yard in length at times. As dad grew older, he would row out several feet away from the end of our dock and let the baited line go to the depth below. Then very carefully, he would let the heavier cloth fishing-line lengthen out as he rowed back to the dock. He then secured the boat in its rightful place. At that time, the dock was built in such a way that it was fashioned like the letter T. He would then tie and secure the heavy fishing pole to the dock behind the raised up T at the end of the dock. At the same time, giving the fish line an extra slack of advance to show that there was not a fish on the line, just yet! Once the deed had been done, he then would proceed to climb up the steps, back up to the cabin and settle in his favorite easy chair. One could see the dock on the beach from the large picture window that graced our home. From there, he would often watch his favorite sports show on TV, while simultaneously checking the fish line with his binoculars. Once the fish line was no longer slack, but rather "tight" in proportion as to what it once was, he knew he had a fish on the line! Then ever so quietly, he would make his way back down the steps to the fishing boat below. Row back out to the direction that the fishing line would take him, and bring in the afternoon catch! I must say, that I don't recommend this type of fishing style, even though it worked quite well for my dad in his elderly years of fishing. I'm sure the game warden would not have approved! Since my beloved dad is no longer with us on this side of the veil, I had to tell his story. Especially, when it contributes to one of the best fish stories of all time and is quite true.

When I was seven years of age my parents chose to sell their home in town and move to the lake full time. Before doing so, they built onto the cabin to include an upstairs attachment. They now had three separate bedrooms and two bathrooms upstairs to accommodate a family of five. I had an older brother and sister who were ten and seven years older than I. The sleeping area down stairs on the main level now became a larger living room space. The area where my crib once was became the long stairs that led up to the new addition.

My father worked in the city about fifty miles away. He commuted back and forth to the Great Northern Railroad yard where he worked as a switchman on the iron rails. He worked for twenty five years before he finally retired with a nice pension. When I was about seven years old I remember dad taking me to the train yard late at night; while a selected few co-workers were secretly present. While there, I was instructed to sit in the main chair of a single front engine; I actually received the rare opportunity to drive the train! It was for a few yards only, but it has been an exhilarating memory that has stayed with me all my life. Because my short legs were not long enough, I had to slip off of the seat to reach the peddle that made the train go forward. I remember the huge light in front of the train illuminating the track in front of us. To this day I have loved trains, especially the antique steam trains. Most of the major cities in America revolve around a train station that provided a better living for the populous of our early ancestors.

My mother worked in a local photography store. Color photos did not exist until later years. Pictures consisted of black and white prints, or on a gold toned canvas. When she moved to the lake she took orders to color the wedding pictures and graduation pictures in oil paint which matched the true colors on the gold tone canvases. She could do that at home and still be a stay-at-home mom while taking care of the family. She had her weekly drive to the photography store in town, to deliver the completed pictures that she had painted. She then collected the new orders coming in to begin again. Most moms did not work when I was young, so my mother was an exception to the rule. However, it afforded us the chance to buy the lake home that we all loved so very much.

The winter's provided us with a different kind of celebration, and that was ice skating. The winters were very cold. The ice on the lake would freeze as much as twelve to eighteen inches thick, so we felt very safe to ice skate on it. Dad would pipe down music of the classical piece of "Swan Lake" as we skated. We even had a small wooden bon fire on the beach surrounded by snow on one occasion while roasting s'mores in the middle of the winter. The road approaching our home was a nice hill that provided us with a good run on the snow sled. We would have a neighborhood party of sledding to be concluded with an indoor gathering of hot chocolate to warm you up, after a day in the cold snow. To this day I remember a sweet neighbor named Helen who's Siamese cat would ride on her shoulders as she sledded down the hill. That cat went everywhere with her. I am a cat lover myself to this day.

As a young child, life was simple and quite happy. I was quite fortunate in my younger years. Maybe it was preparing me for harder times and tasks ahead.

BEING INTRODUCED TO
THE PARA-NORMAL . . . .

I learned at a very young age that there is a spiritual world outside of the physical world. My older siblings were not home on this particular evening. No one was in the house except me and my parents downstairs. When it was time for me to go to bed, my mother walked me upstairs and tucked me in as usual, in the far back bedroom. The bedside table had a light on, so I could look at my comic book before going to sleep. I was too young to actually read at the time, but I enjoyed looking at the colorful pictures. When I finished the book I slipped it under my bed and proceeded to go to sleep. Yet as I laid there in bed I could hear the pages of the comic book turning as if someone was under my bed looking at the book. The space under the bed was too low for an actual person to actually fit underneath it. I was so frightened that I could hardly move. I yelled out the words: "stop it!", but the pages continued to make a rustling noise. I finally got the courage to jump out of bed and run downstairs to tell my mother and father what had happened. My mother took me in her arms and said: "my goodness, your heart is racing". She then carried me back upstairs and reached under the bed for the comic book. Somehow, something had curled one side of the comic book into a very tight roll. The other side of the book lay flat and open. She commented to me that my very small hands could not have created this to happen because it was rolled so tight. She proceeded to put me back to bed with the bedside light still on thankfully, and told me it was time to go to sleep. She then left the room with the comic book in hand to my relief. I laid there shivering in fear, underneath the covers, until I finally fell asleep. We were not religious, so bedtime prayers were not a ritual in our family. This was my first introduction to the spirit world.

THE GHOST IN THE APPLE ORCHARD . . . .

One spring at the age of ten I had a girlfriend from school spend the weekend with me. The next day we took a mile long walk to meet up with another girl our same age, named Debbie. Her family owned one of the local resorts that resided at the end of the lake. She was my closest friend growing up. Debbie's dad had one of the first pin-ball machines in their little resort grocery store. She would open the cash register and grab a few quarters for free. We would play pinball and drink soda to our hearts content. Then of course in the heat of the summer we would swim and water ski. Life was good when I was young I must admit. We didn't have a care in the world. When we spent time together we would often walk to what we called the corner house which was half way between her home and mine. From there we would take turns visiting each other's home. On that particular weekend, my sleepover friend and I decided to visit Debbie at the resort. After calling her, we met at the usual half-way point. From there the three of us kept walking towards the resort. Before it was time to take the right turn towards the lake, Debbie mentioned an apple orchard in the area across from the main road that she wanted to visit. It might just have apples on it this time of year. We were all interested, so instead of heading on our usual route to the lake, we headed left, straight into the deep thick forest. It took us a while to find it, but eventually we found a clearing amongst the tall trees. The area was like an open clearing. It was a rounded piece of land about five acres in diameter. The only trees present were the apple trees situated on the left side of the clearing. This is where we entered the seemingly sacred place. The trees were in full bloom, but no apples had yet taken form. There were no buildings present or any evidence that any other buildings had ever been built there. I was taken in by the oasis of beauty in the middle of this dense forest. Debbie and my school friend were in front of me as we were walking into the orchard area. They were in an active conversation that I was not listening to as we approached the apple orchard. I lagged behind as my eyes drank in the beauty of this natural garden-like open area. The sun was shining through the trees on this beautiful spring filled day. I was questioning in my mind why this area did not have any pine trees growing in it as the orchard area was totally surrounded by pine trees. It seemed rather magical in a way that I could not explain. My friends remained in a deep conversation as we were all the same age and in the same class at school. My eyes went from the full bloomed apple trees on the left of the clearing, to the far right side of the orchard area. At first glance, we were the only ones present in this magical place as I scanned the entire area with my eyes. Several minutes had passed when I was surprised to see a human-like figure standing on top of a raised clay hill or mound. It wasn't there a moment ago. It had on a deep purple and white gown. The figure had a purple hood on that graced its head, but I could not see a face. It looked more spirit-like. The gown had long arms, but I could not see any hands emerge below the sleeves which I thought was strange. The gown reached to the ground but I could not see any feet either. The figure looked very dark within the hood that covered its head. I looked at my friends that were a few yards ahead of me, but they had not taken notice. I looked back at the ghost like figure where it still remained. As I was just about to say something to my friends to alert them; the figure just disappeared in thin air right before my eyes! I was rather shocked to say the least. It took me a minute to digest in my mind what had just happened. I finally told my friends what I had just seen and pointed to the area where the ghost had been standing. We approached the area with caution. When we arrived we noticed that in the middle of a raised clay mound, were a pair of fresh foot prints that looked like the indentions of high heeled shoes. We all had tennis shoes on, that were popular in our day. The raised mound of clay was about four yards in diameter, and about four yards in height. There were no other shoe prints walking to or from these freshly made shoe prints on the top center of the mound where I had seen the figure standing. It was humanly impossible for anyone to jump that far up to the center of the mound, to make the indentations that the foot prints had formed. Even though I was the only one who actually saw the eerie and strange figure, we all saw the foot prints in the place where it had stood just moments prior. The crows were screeching and flying around in circles above our heads. We ran out of there as fast as our ten year old legs could take us! As we continued, my school friend and I saw a misty white angel-like figure floating above us as we left the area. She pointed up at the figure and said: "Look, that is my guardian angel". I had never heard of anyone having a guardian angel to protect them. Both she and Debbie attended the same Catholic Church in a nearby town. Since my family was not religious, I had not been given any pre-training on spiritual matters. We slowed from a dead run to a calmer walk as all three of us saw the protective angel hovering above our heads. I had never seen an angel until that day . . . let alone a ghost! As I gazed upon the pure white orb of the angelic figure floating above us, I felt comforted. A feeling or mantel of peace and safety came over me. The apparition of pure white light faded away as we reached the main road. For many years thereafter the occurrence haunted me as to why it had happened.

The entire experience did not make any sense to me. It was unexplainable. I never told my parents what had happened on that day until years later. I had already learned from an earlier age that things like that were not spoken of.

Several years later, about ten in fact, I returned. This time while in my twenty's I brought a different friend with me for moral support. Interestingly, her name was also Debbi. As we approached the area we were still only half way there. To my surprise we were suddenly startled by a young man running through the woods. As he approached us I noticed that he had the appearance of an American Indian. I recall it was in the peak heat of a hot summer day. The only thing he was wearing was a pair of jeans, no shirt and no shoes. The floor of the forest was densely packed with pine needles and pine cones that would have made it very painful to walk on, let alone run on without any shoes. His long black hair was neatly pulled back into one long braided ponytail that reached down his back to his waistline. He was a fairly young boy about our age in fact. He said that his family had told him there was an ancient burial ground somewhere in the forest in that area, but that he could not find it. He ran off just as quickly as he appeared. Then everything began to make sense. The spirit I saw ten years prior was protecting the burial grounds of that particular ancient Indian tribe! I immediately turned back to tell the young man that it was our intention to visit that same place. I was sure I could find it again. Yet as we turned to look in the direction that he had gone, he was nowhere to be seen. It was impossible for him to have vanished so fast. We should have seen him as he departed. It was a very long way to the main road so he should not have disappeared so soon. Both, my friend Debbi and I were quite perplexed. I think back wondering if it was not a coincidence that we met him on that day for a reason. The lake that I grew up on was named by the American Indians, so they dwelled there long before white men took over the area. We did in fact find the orchard area that we so diligently searched for on that afternoon. The trees were not in bloom as before. No sign of any apples had fallen from the branches. The area looked much the same as did the raised clay mound on the far right side of the orchard. I felt so compelled to return there, searching for answers as to why this happened to us so many years before. This clearing must have been an area where the Indians had once had their encampment in the summer time. I envisioned them having a dwelling place of several T-Pees. Maybe they had cleared this area for a safe place to live at one time. I now felt comforted that now I finally had a logical explanation for the para-normal experience I once had as a young child.

More than anything, it also confirmed to me once again that there is a spiritual world separate from the physical world. And that life must go on after we die; leaving our physical remains behind. My friends and I still remember the experiences that we had that very first time we visited the so called orchard versus burial grounds. We are now in our middle aged years. Some memories never fade. They leave lasting impressions on your mind forever.

EVERYDAY MIRACLES . . . .

There's an old saying that says: "A cat has nine lives". Sometimes that saying can apply to our own personal life if it's not our time to cross over to the other side of the veil.

When I was sixteen I took on a job as an Avon Lady and sold their products door to door in the area where I lived. The world was a much safer place in my younger years. Even though I was quite shy in school, it seemed to help me gain confidence. Most people liked the product, so ninety nine percent of the people I met gave me an order. It also gave me the gift of gab and I sort of became what they call a "Chatty-Cathy". I met the nicest people all over the lake where I grew up. I was lucky enough to be able to drive my mother's car, so I had transportation. One day however I was confronted with a very close call that I thought for sure would take away my life. I was driving on one of the back roads on the opposite side of the lake. An old man was driving on the wrong side of the dirt road directly at me. It happened so fast that I didn't have time to react. When he was about three inches way, I closed my eyes just before impact, knowing that we were going to have a head on car to car collision. Within seconds I opened my eyes and to my astonishment the very same car was now about a block away from me. I quickly pulled off to the side of the road and watched him drive by. I just sat there for a few minutes quite stunned and astounded that my life had just been spared. I knew without a doubt that there is definitely a higher power in charge.

What actually happened? Did God give me an instantaneous premonition that spared my life? To this day, I really don't know.

Another time, I was driving behind a truck that was pulling a boat trailer with a very large speed boat in tow. For some reason I had a strange thought that the boat was not secured well enough to the trailer, yet there was no visible evidence for me to think this. Intuitively I slowed way down to place a large distance between us. Just as soon as I did so, the boat slid off of its trailer towards me at the speed of fifty miles an hour. It then turned over to its right side as it slid into the ditch right in front of me. If I hadn't slowed down, just moments before, I would have had an enormous boat crashing down on my front window. Again my life was spared.

So if is not your time to go home to the borders of God's kingdom, be aware that every day miracles do happen. I do believe in guardian angels.

Just recently I once again walked away from the potential knock at deaths door. I was driving home from work at the usual time close to midnight. Since I work evening shift at a nearby hospital, I am use to driving home in the dark of night. As usual I was in my own little world while listening to my favorite late night talk radio show. There were no cars in front of me, so I thought I had the road to myself on this particular night. I was driving the expected speed limit of 60 miles an hour when all of a sudden I was rear-ended by a force from behind, causing me to lunge forward at a faster speed than I was going. I immediately glanced up into my rear view mirror to find that nothing was behind me. The next thing I saw was a motorcycle on its side flying past me; sparks flying everywhere without a driver! Come to find out later, there were two motorcycles that approached me that night, both driven by drunk drivers. The one that hit me directly from behind then swerved to the left taking out his buddy next to him; causing both drivers to lose control of their motor bikes. Both men went flying through the air to land in the grass land between the east and west bound traffic. If there had been a cement barrier between these apposing lanes, the outcome could have been much different for all three of us. Thank God they both lived! While they were both taken to the hospital in their perspective aid cars, I drove home with only a few dents. My only adversity was the adrenaline pumping through my veins that caused me to stay awake all night. Once again I seemed to be protected somehow.

IN YOUR LIFE TIME, FOLLOW THE LIGHT, NOT THE DARKNESS . . . .

. . . . These words were spoken to me telepathically many years ago. I was a very young girl at the age of fifteen. It happened unexpectantly; the whole experience took me by surprise. As an adult looking back, I realize now, that I had a visionary, (out of body), near-death experience. I grew up in an all American typical family, except that we were not religious. We did not attend church often, except on an occasional holiday service at the non-denominational church nearby.

I was seeking for answers that consisted of a spiritual nature as most children do at that young age. I had been fasting for about two weeks, eating very little while ingesting only small amounts of water. I am sure my body was very dehydrated.

My mother had purchased a bible for me to read, even though we did not attend church regularly. The bible she gave me was the King James Version with a pretty white leather cover. I remember reading in the New Testament the words: "The Father, The Son, and the Holy Spirit." I had accepted and believed in the Father and the Son> the anointing of Christ Jesus in my mind and heart as saviour; yet I was still compelled to search for something deeper than just words in a book. I had fasted for two weeks prior; soul searching in a diligent quest for answers. I prayed on my knees at my bedside in private, in hopes that God would reveal himself to me. I remember being determined; almost angry in a challenging way. I wasn't going to give up, until I got an answer DIRECTLY from God. There was really no one else in my life to ask or confide in. I prayed on my knees at my bedside before going to bed, asking that God would reveal himself to me personally. I then got into bed and opened my bible to the words: "The Holy Spirit". I comprehended and knew what the Father and the Son meant, but I did not know what the Holy Spirit was. So I thought to myself . . . . "Father, what is the Holy Spirit"? To my surprise there was a telepathic response to my question. It was NOT an audible response in a physical sense, but that of telepathic thought transference. The message was very powerful, which resonated through my entire being. I literally felt the vibration of His words through every cell of my body.

His words were:

"I WILL ANSWER YOU, BUT I WILL ANSWER YOU IN MY OWN TIME".

The alchemy of God's words vibrated like thunder through my soul and heart. Without a doubt, I knew that I had heard the actual thoughts of God! Not in a quiet way, but in a very powerful baritone resonance. His great love and peacefulness flooded through my inner being. A profound and complete trust overcame me; I knew somehow that His words were like a contract. I felt an inner comfort and satisfaction that I had found an answer to my deep soul searching. I knew without a doubt that He would keep His word to me and answer my question. Yet I pondered on His words: "IN MY OWN TIME" . . . . I thought to myself, "how strange", "That could be in five minutes from now, or five years from now." I didn't completely understand the meaning of His words at such a young age. I didn't realize then, that it would take a lifetime to discover God's full answer.

However a feeling of complete comfort and love filled my inner being with a trustful heart. I was satisfied that someday I would get an answer. I put my bible down on the end table next to my bed, and turned off the light. As I put my head down on my pillow, I immediately felt a presence. My room was pitch black. The window shade kept the moon light from shining in. The bedroom door was completely shut. I sat straight up, knowing that someone or something was in my room. My head was no longer on the pillow as I sat upright in bed. The presence I sensed was as big as an adult person, but I could barely see its source due to my darkened room. Yet I could hear and feel a presence of some sort. Why I didn't turn on my bedside lamp I don't know. It all happened so fast! I was so frightened; I just closed my eyes in total fear. This presence seemed to have substance because I could hear it approaching my bed. It continued to come closer until it stood right next to me. I then felt a gentle touch on the top of my head and another on the top of my right shoulder. The touch was not a physical touch, but that of a spiritual nature. I felt an inner shower of light surge through my inner soul and body. A cool sensation of energy cascaded through me like an inner shower cleansing my body from inside out. Every portion of my inner soul from the top of my head to the tip my toes were being infused with the feeling of living light. I felt like I was being baptized with the energy of living waters in an etheric down pouring inside my soul. As this was occurring I was also given a vision as my eyes remained closed. Yet I felt like I was a part of that vision. My fear had totally dissipated by now. My eyes were still completely closed, yet I was seeing in my mind's eye a beautiful forest. It was like I was in a different dimension or space of time. I felt like I was outside of my body. Within this forest, I noticed that the trees were the tallest trees I had ever seen. The colors were very vivid. I looked up but I could not see the sky due to the crowed density of leaves and branches. Only a few shafts of light were streaming down through the forest. As my attention was drawn to the ground, I saw a small stream of very clear water. Next to it was a delicate flower with four deep purple petals. It seemed to be reaching upward in a struggling effort to obtain the few streams of sunlight it could possibly find. Its stem was at least twelve inches long. It had sprouted upward, yet fallen back to the ground in its quest to reach the light. It then continued to grow upward in search for the sparse precious rays of scarce sunlight that it could find. I noticed that the stem of the flower was very delicate as a gentle breeze caused it to sway back and forth with the wind. How delicate and vulnerable it was! Somehow I knew that I was being shown, that my own quest for light was likened to this flower. I glanced back to the small stream of water that was trickling through the floor of the forest. I noticed how clear the water was as I crouched down to get a closer look. The water was pure and alive, different than I had ever seen before, crystal clear. Then something strange happened. I felt like a part of me had melded with the water of the stream. I could feel the living waters of the stream inside my soul body again, showering down from the top of my head to the tip of my toes. I felt one with the living waters of light. I could actually feel the cool sensations of the water flowing through my soul body. As the stream of water continued to flow through the forest, its source blended with a larger body of water. It then flowed into a full-fledged river. The currents of the water were very strong and forceful. I could hear the rushing noise of a waterfall in my inner ear. The strong currents overcame me with so much discomfort that it caused me to open my eyes. I couldn't withstand the powerful energy that was surging through my inner being. The vision of the forest vanished and I found myself immersed within a cloud of white pure light. The light was not of this world. It was the brightest light I had ever seen, but it didn't hurt my eyes. My soul had traveled to a different dimension. It was as if I was between worlds. I found myself within a cumulous cloud of pure energy. The light emitted the alchemy of pure unconditional love. I felt like I was in a space of pure loving bliss. There are no adequate words within the human language that can fully explain this blissful state that I was experiencing. I was in total awe of this pure light and love; I was completely speechless. The next thing that happened, I saw a spiritual being reach out to me through this cloud like substance. The spirit that I saw had a pure white gown on with long belled sleeves. He reached out to me with his right arm and hand as if waiting for me to place my hand in his. I knew somehow that if I had done so, I could have crossed over to my spiritual home. It was an invitation to step into a heavenly dimension different than mine own. I started to reach out my right arm to place my hand in His. Yet as I began to do so, my physical heart contracted with a sharp piercing pain. I drew back my hand and covered my heart with my palm. I then thought these words:

> "Father, forgive me, but I am not ready to come home yet".

To my surprise, the white cloud completely dissipated and disappeared. So did the blissful state of unconditional love that I was completely immersed in just moments prior. Instead I found myself surrounded by complete darkness. Yet this darkness was profoundly dense, without any signs of life or sound. You couldn't even hear a pin drop. Looking back, I now know that I was in a space that the bible calls, "The valley of the shadow of death". Another name for it is called the void. There were no signs of life what-so-ever to my knowledge, just pure darkness, immersed in complete silence. It was as if my soul was one with the darkness. It was so different from the alchemy of light and love. Then all of a sudden I felt like my soul had returned to my physical body. I reached over and turned on the bedside lamp next to my bed. I just sat there dumbfounded and speechless as to what I had just experienced. I thought to myself:

"What is the point of all this"?

Immediately I received a telepathic communication that said to me:

"IN YOUR LIFETIME, FOLLOW THE LIGHT, NOT THE DARKNESS".

Once again, I heard words from Gods communicating thoughts within my inner being, NOT audible.

I sat there pondering on these words as to their full meaning. I had not only heard these words telepathically, I had just experienced these words as if they were living words of experience within my soul. I was given a great gift of actually being at-one-ment within the light, to include an at-one-ment within total darkness. I felt the alchemy of both experiences within my inner soul. I had experienced the osmosis of being ONE with the light, then the osmosis of being ONE with the darkness. The LIGHT was filled with LIFE and pure LOVE, with a sense of goodness. The darkness seemed void of all life and in a space of nothingness, only dead silence.

The beautiful feeling of unconditional love I had just experienced was now just a memory. It was not ONE within my soul to the strength and magnitude that it was, just a few moments before. As I sat there pondering on the experience, I thought to myself:

"I will seek for this light, even if it takes me a lifetime to find it".

I knew then that the HOLY SPIRIT is the pure energy of unconditional love. I turned back to the small desk lamp by my bed; turned it off and settled into bed. I was more than satisfied that I had received an answer to my soul searching. Strangely enough, I didn't speak to anyone about this extraordinary experience for many years. Yet the experience was branded on my soul and inner being like it happened yesterday. I will remember this to the day that I die and finally cross over to my spiritual home. To this day I am often home-sick for the blissful state of unconditional love that I had experienced on that day.

When I do cross over, don't cry for me, because it will be a happy day of celebration for me to return to my spiritual home. There is nothing to fear if you follow the light when you do cross over from this dimension into the next. When it's your time to be called home, ask God to help you cross over into the light while escorting you back to our spiritual beginnings. We are only guests within this physical body for a short time. We are here to learn the lessons of life that cross our path on our journey back home.

Just recently I have learned that my good friend Debbi, who had accompanied me to the ancient burial grounds while we were in our early twenties, had also heard the telepathic words of God. She was only five years of age at the time. As an adult, she now has a Doctorate Degree in teaching. The telepathic words that were given to her were, "BE STILL AND KNOW THAT I AM GOD." She expressed to me, that when she received these words, she had not realized this phrase was actually written in the bible until she was much older. I asked her if she had felt the power of His resonance within her inner soul; she agreed that her experience felt much the same as mine.

Ten years went by before I spoke of this experience to anyone. I was inspired to do so even more so after reading a book by Dr. Raymond Moody called: "Life after Life". For some reason my mother-in-law had given me a copy of his book. Yet she was not aware of my experience as a young teenager. Within his research of "near-death experiences", better known as NDE'S he explains that there are up to ten different commonalities that people sometimes experience when they have a near-death experience. I realized that I had experienced six out of these ten possible signs.

I also recommend a book called "Proof of Heaven" by Dr. Eben Alexander. He did not believe in near-death experiences as a man of science until he had one himself. Being a neuro-brain surgeon he had previously explained these phenomena as hallucinations of the brain. Since he had experienced being in a coma from bacterial meningitis which is an inflammation of the brain's outer cortex, it was impossible for his physical brain to conjure up the soul consciousness his near-death experience provided him. Thousands of people have had near-death or visionary experiences separate from their physical body.

BEING FILLED WITH
THE HOLY SPIRIT

Being filled with the Holy Spirit is like taking a shower inside your soul, likened to the **living water** that the bible verses speak about. The **light** of Christ is a very **powerful** force.

This bible scripture explains it quite well:

> (NKJV) John 7: Verse 37> "On the last day, that great day of the feast, Jesus stood and cried out, saying, "If anyone thirsts, let him come to Me and drink."
>
> Verse 38> "He who believes in Me [Jesus], as the Scripture has said, **out of his heart will flow rivers of living water."**
>
> Verse 39> "But this He spoke concerning the Spirit, whom those believing in Him would receive; **for the Holy Spirit was not yet given, because Jesus was not yet glorified.**
>
> Verse 42> "Has not the Scripture said that the Christ comes from the seed of David and from the town of Bethlehem, where David was?"

I wish to interject here that this previous scripture speaks of the **pre-existence of the soul of Christ before Jesus was anointed.**

> (NKJV) John 4: Verse 14> "but whoever drinks of the water that I shall give him will never thirst. **But**

the water that I shall give him will become in him a fountain of water springing up into everlasting life."

(NKJV) Act 2: Verse 38> "Then Peter said to them, "Repent, and let every one of you be baptized in the name of Jesus Christ for the remission of sins; and you shall receive the gift of the Holy Spirit."

(NKJV) Luke 24: Verse 46> "Then He said to them, "Thus it is written, and thus it was necessary for the Christ to suffer and to rise from the dead the third day, Verse 47> "and that repentance and remission of sins should be preached in His name to all nations, beginning at Jerusalem.

Verse 48> "And you are witnesses of these things. Verse 49> "Behold, I send the Promise of My Father upon you; but tarry in the city of Jerusalem until you are endued with **power** from on high."

These biblical scriptures give us a detailed review of the powerful force of the Holy Spirit. Because Jesus was filled with the anointing of Christ, He was the living manifestation of the Holy Spirit who walked on this earth plane; **Jesus was and is the living Christ.**

The biblical word of God explains that the Christ became flesh and walked among us. Read as follows:

(NKJV) John Chapter 1: Verse 12> "But as many as received Him, to them He gave the right to become children of God, to those who believe in His name: Verse 13> "who were born, not of blood, nor of the will of the flesh, nor of the will of man, but of God. Verse 14> **"And the Word became flesh and dwelt among us, and we beheld His glory, the glory as of the only begotten of the Father, full of grace and truth."**

LIFE GOES ON AS A YOUNG ADULT / TRANSMIGRATION OF SOULS

After this happened to me my life as a teenager continued, but with a greater awareness about life. I moved to town and lived with my grandparents when I was eighteen. I started attending a church nearby my home called the Episcopal Church. The pomp and circumstance was much like that of the Catholic Church with one major exception. The priests could marry and have a normal family life. The traditions of the church were much the same with the kneeling benches when we were in prayer. We often recited the apostle's creed at almost every service. I once sat by a young lady that commented that her Aunt had a rare book that survived several centuries back in time. She said that it had the Apostle's Creed in it, but that it recited differently than what it states in this century. She said that during the crusades while they were burning books, this particular book escaped the burnings. It was kept safe and hidden away. She said that the phrase in this book stated:

"I believe in the transmigration of souls".

Instead of, I believe in the universal Catholic Church.

I responded, "What does that mean?" She answered back, "Reincarnation". I said, "Oh, I don't believe in that." We never spoke again, but I kept her words in my memory for safe keeping. Later in my life I began to question the validity of her words, ... "the transmigration of souls".

DREAMS . . . .

. . . . When I was only five years old I would have a recurring dream that seemed like a nightmare to me. It was the same dream over and over. Each time I would wake up crying. Within this dream I was a full grown woman with an infant in my arms. I recall having on a black taffeta dress that was gathered at my small waistline; it continued down in full dress to reach the floor. My black shoes buckled up above my ankles. There was delicate detailed white lace around the end of my long black taffeta sleeves. My long brown hair was pulled up in a bun on the top of my head. I had within my arms a child that could not have been more than a year old at the most. I knew within my dream that I was in a place called Paris. I viewed this dream as if I was one within this woman, not as an observer. Then everything would go dark as if something heavy had fallen over us to take our lives away. I remember thinking I was going to die along with my child within the dream. At this point, I would wake up crying. Even at the age of five I wondered why I would dream that I was a full grown person; with a baby in my arms that I knew was my own? Later in my life I would realize it was a soul memory deep within my subconscious.

In my early thirties I had a spontaneous one-time experience of what they call Knundalini. This happens when the pranic-breath of the Holy Spirit is released within ones inner soul body. I could actually see my aura with what is referred to as the "third eye"; the intuitive eye which resides in front of the pineal and pituitary glands within our endocrine system.

I will reserve this chapter later in my book. This is when I began to question the validity of reincarnation.

If you do a history search of some of the early founding fathers of Christianity called the Gnostic Christians, you will find that they too taught reincarnation. Gnosis means: 'to know'> direct knowledge of the Divine. The ancient teaching of the Jewish Kabbalah explains the metamorphosis of the soul from one physical life to another. It takes an eternity to perfect one's soul from one level to the next.

I have read that the ancient order of Cather's in France also believed in reincarnation. However, they also taught that:

> **"The chain of reincarnation was broken, when one experienced the anointing of the Holy Spirit of Christ within their inner soul body.**
>
> **They taught the importance of the "second birth", the birth of the soul."**

Biblical history explains that the disciples fled for their lives after Jesus was crucified on the cross. I have read that some of the followers of Jesus eventually left Rome to reside in Upper Egypt.

Leather bindings of additional books containing secret Gnostic Gospels were found in Upper Egypt within a cave in the year 1945 inside of a sealed clay pot near the city of Nag Hammadi carefully preserved. Though some of these original texts were destroyed; those which still remain are now kept and preserved at the Nag Hammadi Library by the Egyptian government. You can obtain this information in English if you look it up on the Wikipedia.org. Once there, you can access many of the original gospels of our Christian forefathers. When searching for the Gnostic Gospels, seek out the alphabetical download of information online. From this site, one can find additional gospels to include the Gospel of Thomas and many others.

I have no proof of the "transmigration of souls" except for my own past life memories and what I have read in different texts. I heard the young girl at the Episcopal Church mention it to me so many years long ago; I must admit it did make a major impact on my life. I would have loved to have seen the book that her Aunt still housed within her possessions.

If I were to have lived in the time of the Christian crusades I would have most likely been burned at the stake to even mention the word reincarnation. From what I have read in different texts and historic literature, during 553 AD, the Fifth Enumerical Council, also known as the council of Constantinople sanctioned a meeting. This meeting's purpose was to conjoin the political agenda of their day with those of religious mind, within the church of Christianity.

They desired to take control of both church and state to form into one controlled thought. This meeting was ruled by the Emperor Justinian the First, who succeeded Constantine. History explains that even though Constantine had embraced most of the original truths of Christianity the Emperor Justinian who later succeeded him did not. I have read that during that time in history, Justinian arrested the Pope in Rome because he refused to attend his political meeting with the purpose to bring forth church and state as one.

I have read in historical accounts during Justinian's reign that the monks were forced to sign new laws or edicts that condemned specific Gnostic teachings; these included not only the **pre-existence** of one's inner **soul**, but the **resurrection of the soul**, not of the flesh. Also condemned was the teaching that **God the Father is invisible and transcendent.**

Those who did not sign the new laws were punished and accused of being heretics. Some were tortured for all to see.

Some of these horrible acts of violence and cruelty were performed for public eye to view first hand. I have read that many were brutally beaten with whips. Others hung from their feet with their bodies hanging downward to the ground. The popular peace sign that we know in our present day is actually a symbol depicting how some of our early Church forefathers were hung upside down and killed. Some early Christians were brought into the citadel to be attached by wild tigers that were previously starved, then let loose so they could mar their broken bodies for sustenance. This was a harsh reminder that Roman rule had been placed above spiritual law. It was not popular to be an early Gnostic Christian.

Yet somehow, our early believers hid the deeper mysteries of Christianity which we now have access to; thanks to the government of Egypt; now preserved within the confines of the Nag Hammadi Library.

The apostle Peter in the first century A.D. had previously written letters to the followers of early Christianity throughout the known world of that region; Gospels by other disciples were established as well, written and preserved for all to admonish. The Church of Ephesus was the hub of many of the first forefathers. To follow were other temples once ruled by pagan Gods now displaced with the ONE GOD of the Universe. These seven churches of Revelation were those of Ephesus, Smyrna, Pergamos, Thyatira, Sardis, Philadelphia, and that of Laodiciea. The true precepts of Christianity that were once taught were now taken over by Roman occupation by the middle and end of the fifth century AD. The monks were displaced if they did not conform to the new laws laid down by the Emperor Justinian; their positions of high standings were filled with those who bended to the wills of political rule within the Roman government. Some of the deeper mysteries of God and the Holy Spirit were displaced with lesser values; lost and hidden.

Once again leaving humanity within their ranks to dwell in the ignorance of spiritual darkness; separate from the whole truth of the totality of Christ's original teachings. Our present day's world has adopted many of the watered down versions of spiritual domain under ancient Rome's political influence, even up to modern time.

The ultimate political goal was to end the belief in reincarnation in orthodox Christianity; calling those who did with the accusations of heresy. The first council of Nicaea previously convened in the year 325 AD with the purpose to eradicate teachings that it is possible to **seek direct union with God within the Holy Spirit.** The political powers of the time wanted complete rule.

REINCARNATION
GILGULL HESHAMOT

(NKJV): Job 33: 21-25 refers to our "flesh becoming young again".

Our soul is formed from the nature of creation. Like the natural seasons of the earth, from spring representing birth, to summer, then fall, then winter. Spring comes once again in full circle, creating season after season, completing the different cycles of nature.

Reincarnation has been described in ancient time as the transmigration of souls after death in the esoteric teachings of the Kabbalah. Another description refers to what is called: GILGUL HESHAMOT which translates as ("cycles of the soul"). Some of our early Christian fathers accepted these teachings that describe the rectification of the soul.

Some believed that our soul returns time and time again with different incarnations throughout the course of time until our soul matures.

Others taught that once we are filled with the Holy Spirit and receive the forgiveness of sins that the anointing of the cosmic Christ provides, this cycle is broken; we return once again to the primordial source from where our soul originated at the end of this present life.

This master plan explains a greater scope of personalized trial by error until one's soul is rectified to perfection. **This view displaces the thought of living only one life before being sent to heaven or to hell for eternity of time.**

(NKJV) John 14: Verse 2> "In My Father's house are many mansions; if it were not so, I would have told you. I go to prepare a place for you."

Some believe that when we cross over at the end of this present life we will be surrounded by those of like mind: being placed in one of the seven levels of heaven until one reaches a personal light body that resides closest to the throne of the source of God. The goal is to be filled with the light and love of Christ within our body, mind, and soul to its very fullest potential; our ultimate goal is to be equally balanced in all three.

The Church of Christendom that we know today in our present time was largely molded by the Emperor Justinian in the fifth century A.D., displacing some of these deeper mysteries of the Holy Spirit.

These deeper mysteries that Jesus taught his disciples were in smaller circles, not shared during the general public address to the masses. Many of these private teachings can be found in the gospels that are housed in the Nag Hammadi library of Egypt. Other writings that were not included in the New Testament are those of the Apocrypha and the discovery of the Dead Sea Scrolls. Fortunately these early works of scriptures that have recently been discovered in the 1900's are now accessible online for anyone interested in further self-study.

Other bible verses that suggest reincarnation is in the book of Matthew, and also the book of Mark.

(NKJV) Matthew, Chapter 16: 13-14:
Verse 13> "When Jesus came into the region of Caesarea Philippi, He asked His disciples, saying, "Who do men say that I, the Son of Man, am?"

Verse 14> "So they said, "Some say John the Baptist, some Elijah, and others Jeremiah or one of the prophets.""

(NKJV) Mark, Chapter 8: 27-30:

Verse 27> "Now Jesus and His disciples went out to the towns of Caesarea Philippi; and on the road He asked His disciples, saying to them, "Who do men say that I am?""

Verse 28> "So they answered, "John the Baptist; but some say, Elijah; and others, one of the prophets.""

Some believe that these previous scriptures suggest the pre-existence of one's soul and reincarnation. In my understanding, it takes more than one life time to learn all the lessons of the soul in the course of eternity. This does not mean that we are not accountable in this present life time to learn good works. The age old saying, 'what you reap is what you sow', can be true today in our present day lives. This parable can be likened to the teachings of cause and effect.

KARMA . . . .

Karma is the same as cause and effect. The one place you can find it referred to in the Bible is:

> (NKJV) Ecclesiastic 11: Verse 1 > "Cast your bread upon the waters, For you will find it after many days."

It refers to bread being cast upon the waters, knowing that it will return to you several days later. Symbolic words to reflect the meaning of karma. Some believe this verse is also suggestive of reincarnation because of the phrase 'several days'.

Each thought and every action we take will not only affect our own life but the lives of others. When our soul crosses over to return back to the source, we go through a life review. We see our whole life pass before us in panoramic viewing. Except we see it in a different light. We not only see ourselves; we feel the effects and feelings of everyone else who has crossed our path during our life on earth.

I have learned that **how we live out this present life reflects and determines the quality of life we (may) have in our next incarnation.**

This observation however is not always the case when you look at the life of Jesus who was persecuted even though he was blameless and lived a life of doing the Father's will to help the human race. He faced a very spiritually dark world when he walked on this earth during his life time; his goal was to bring light to those who were willing to listen, regardless of the price he had to pay.

Yet it is so very important to choose well during this present life's incarnation; and to deal with what-so-ever twists and turns our life has to offer this time around to the best of our ability. We often learn by experience. Some learn faster than others. Some learn by example. It's important to humble ourselves in prayer and ask for forgiveness. Because Jesus is the Christ anointed, we can ask for forgiveness through Him in prayer. Through him, we can also ask to be filled with the Holy Spirit of God's love and light.

Learn how to turn your tribulations into a better way of living until you find a harmonious outcome. Time heals everything in due time. Give life a chance to recalibrate itself. Nature is self-healing as is your soul, for our soul is also part of nature. It is often through tribulations that our soul matures.

There is a blessing in coming into a new life with a clean slate; a chance for a new beginning. The pre-existence of our soul cannot be comprehended by our physical human conscientiousness until we have elevated ourselves to a higher spiritual understanding.

The belief in reincarnation has helped me view life differently. I no longer feel sorry for myself that my present life is not perfect. I don't compare myself to others. I know without a doubt that I have an eternity to experience life. Our soul's evolution is aimed towards maturity, into the spiritual light of basic goodness and good will, not only to ourselves but towards our fellow man. These precepts will reflect back to us in due time from life to life until our soul has learned all its lessons in this material form. Our ultimate goal is to perfect the light of the Universal Father/Mother God-Source within our body, mind, and soul until we transcend the need to return. The true home of our soul is that of spirit. The blue jewel called Earth is a rich opportunity to perfect our learning process with personal experience and personal enlightenment. Spiritual enlightenment is there when you are ready to seek it out. Jacob's ladder is a parable that depicts the symbolic story which teaches us the lessons of life one step at a time from one level to the next until we reach the heavenly realm. We learn one day at a time through trial and error, these being looked upon as opportunities to learn. The challenge is to turn these trials and tribulations into a positive attitude, or a directional change of one's life course. Results of our past actions with the cause and affect theory may help us understand our present situation in this life. With the universal law that states that 'what-so-ever a man sows, so shall he reap'. We earn our rightful place and position in life's journey by the fruits of our labor, possibly from those of a past incarnations rather than a present one; or until we learn what it is that we need to perfect within our own soul.

Half of the human race accepts reincarnation as fact. Much of the populous of western mind has swallowed the teachings that discount the ancient truths of our forefathers due to the ignorance of religious history; these teachings were created and maneuvered in such a way that ancient Roman rulers dictated that anyone who believed in this way of thinking was accused of being a heretic. If you do a study of the history of ancient Roman rule and their control over the beginnings of the Church, you will find out and discover what they did to heretics under their jurisdiction. Many of them were tortured, or put to death.

Since my own spiritual experience, I have read several books on near death experiences. I have also read the work of Dr. Michael Newton with his ground breaking work with life between lives. In his book: "Journey of Souls", and "Destiny of Souls", he basically explains that we are on an eternal journey to perfect the evolution of our soul. I do not believe that we come back as the family's favorite pet however. According to his work with past life regression, our soul is in pre-existence before we are born into this earth life we have chosen. No one forces us to come; we come at our own choosing and learn at our own pace. Though some of us remember our past lives on a subconscious level in a dream state, there are many who do not have this memory; or they often discount it, not realizing what it means. When our physical body is in its infancy, our soul blends with the human body; we often do not remember our past lives. Our physical conscientious mind has no memory of it what-so-ever because our present human life has not experienced any other life except this present existence.

Until your soul begins the path to a spiritual awakening, past life memories will lie dormant. Dr. Newton's study of past life regression taps into the deeper memories of our soul. We sometimes bring sub-conscientious memories of past life traumas into this present life. It is part of the memory within our soul's aura. Such as the fear of drowning or an unexplained pain that has no physical bearing in this life.

"DON'T JUDGE A PERSON UNTIL YOU WALK IN THEIR MOCCASINS."

This was one of my grandmother's favorite sayings.

I have learned that it is important that we do not judge one another within the circle of people who touch our lives. Since some people choose to have a fairly easy life this time around, while others may be working on a more challenging life time. I have also read that when we leave this earth plane we will eventually have an opportunity to view the life we have just lived, to see what we had learned this time around. No one judges us: we ultimately judge ourselves. That's why we often return until we learn our lessons well. Some believe that pre-destined occurrences are set before your present life's path at different stages in life, so lessons of the soul can help us individually advance to maturity.

My grandmother also explained to me, that many years ago in the state of Kansas, one of my relatives married a Cherokee woman. So it is suspected that a portion of my blood line is from the indigenous nation of the Cherokee Indians. I know what it means when many tribes speak about the LAND of the EARTH being SACRED ground. Nature has a pristine holiness about it when you see the beauty of it. Whether it is a beautiful spring morning with wild flowers in full bloom; or the first fallen snow of the quiet winter blanketed in pure white snow, it's in harmony with the spirit of God's love. I view the land at the lake where I grew up as sacred. I felt ONE with nature on a daily basis in my younger years. I lived predominately outside during my waking hours during the summer months. To become ONE with creation is the same as being ONE with the God source. To me as I personally have experienced, God is pure etheric energy, outside of our physical five senses.

AMERICAN INDIAN
SPIRITUAL VISION . . . .

When I was much older while in my early forties I attended a church meeting where they had a teacher by the name of Almine. She spoke about the teachings of the indigenous American Indians with the music of the drum. She took us through a visualized meditation to show us how to express our love to the Earth whose soul name is Gaiya she explained. The purpose of this meditation was to surround the Earth with our prayers of Love and well-being. The goal was to have what the American Indians refer to as a spirit quest. She placed soft pleasant music on with the faint sound of a beating drum. The room was filled with about 400 people. The spirit of God's Love permeated the room. She had us imagine with our mind, our heart opening up like the bud of a sunflower to full bloom. To then step out of our hearts like an orb that looked like the moon. Our purpose was to soul travel to the Milky Way in a guided meditation. She explained it was very important to pray for protection with our guardian angels before going on a spirit quest, so I felt safe after our group prayer. To my surprise, I actually soul traveled out of my body while totally conscientious. I remember having dreams of flying when I was a very small child, yet never had I actually left my body this freely since my near-death vision. I think this technique could be somewhat the same as remote viewing which is quite popular with some sections of the military. As we visualized the Earth from a distance above, we were led to circle the Earth with our love and healing thoughts. She directed us to the top of the north-pole then around the Earth, to rest there once again. The next step was to rest on the equator and to circle around again with the same intent. I felt so free like a small bird flying around with the orb of my spirit body. Within my own curiosity, I wondered what it would be like to go back to the top of the north-pole, then to soul travel right through the middle of the Earth to the south-pole, so I did. I did the same on the equator traveling from east to west right through the middle of the earth's etheric soul body. The Earth has a soul just like we do, but within a much grander scale of course. As I did this, I centered myself in the center of the Earth. In my mind's eye I could see the pillar of light energy that is formed from the north to the south-pole. It illuminated with a beautiful white light of glowing energy. There to the side of the glowing energy I was approached by a very old white haired grandmotherly woman.

Since this day, I have personally been told from a Hawaiian Shaman that she is referred to as the "Guardian of the Earth". I have also spoken to American Indians who call her "Grandmother Earth", others refer to her as Gaia.

She stood up from her resting place as if she was in deep meditation; she then slowly stood up and walked towards me to face me. To my surprise, she telepathically spoke to me in a very ancient language that I had never heard before. I remember thinking to myself, "I don't understand." There was a long pause of silence, followed by telepathic words that were now in my own language. The first thing she told me was my soul name, which is very sacred to me. I since have been told by an American Indian that this name is never meant to be shared with the rest of the world. And somehow, I seemed to know this within my own heart of inner wisdom. The greatest form of wisdom is to "know" that something is true by experiencing it firsthand.

Grandmother Earth then telepathically communicated these words to me personally:

"My people have forgotten me, so I reach out to all the people of the land."

She then placed two golden nuggets, one in each of my palms; she instructed me that these gold stones symbolized my two children. She also gave me a set of white moccasin shoes with red beads forming a bird on the top of each shoe. I then saw the full dress of pure white feathers, like the wings of an angel, grace my back side. It was communicated to me that this was the symbol of angelic protection, not only for my children but also for me. I thanked her for her gifts while wanting to stay longer. Yet Almine was calling us back from the guided meditation to rejoin within the heart flame of our own physical body. Though Almine's meditation did not include what I had just experienced personally; I cherished what Grandmother Earth showed me. The most profound is that our **Beloved Earth has a soul and is a sentient being.**

We need to stop hurting her. I have read that the oil within the Earth is likened to the blood in our own veins. Her gold and precious metals help keep the north and south-pole in perfect electromagnetic balance.

Be mindful of our environment and the natural balance of nature. There is something to be said for the ancient indigenous tribes around the world who have lived in harmony with Mother Nature before the white man has taken over the face of the earth. We as a people need to return to the ancient ways of harmony with the earth. I also question some of the pesticides that are being used to dust the crops; changing the molecular balance of our food source. I question many things that seem to be polluting our precious Mother Earth. I encourage my closest friends to go organic especially when one is pregnant.

"YOU DON'T HAVE TO GO TO CHURCH TO BE A GOOD CHRISTIAN"

This is what my own Grandmother, whom we called Nanny, would often say to me. I think what she really meant was that you don't have to go to church to be a good person. The Bible explains that, for indeed, the kingdom of God is within you.

> Read: (NKJV): Luke 17: Verse 21> "nor will they say, 'See here!' or 'See there!' For indeed, the kingdom of God is within you."

Through the years I have gone to many different churches. I have learned many truths. During my near-death vision, I was never told which religion or which church to attend. It only specified to

"FOLLOW THE LIGHT, NOT THE DARKNESS".

I think it's different for every person who walks the earth. I've learned that you cannot contain God in one religion. He reaches out to all cultures, to all Nations of the Human race and to all skin tones. We are all from the same essence from the God-Source within our soul body. We are made in God's likeness. Our soul body stems from the pure energy of etheric consciousness from the Father of the universe and the Mother of the universe. Our outer body is the result from the evolution of our human physical form on this earth plane. Our physical body and our soul body are separate, yet blended into one.

Since I was surrounded by Christianity in my own experience, this is the avenue that the God-Source reached out to teach me the truth that I first sought out. I wish to say that I have also kept an open mind. I have learned spiritual truths from many nations from around the globe. I would say that I am more spiritual than religious at this stage of my life. I consider myself a Gnostic Christian more so than a fundamentalist. I accept the ancient truths that were once taught when Jesus walked the earth.

For me, it was the baptism of the Holy Spirit that awakened my soul to the Love of God. I personally do accept that the human being called Jesus Christ was a conduit for God's truth, Love, and Holy Spirit, and that the Father God chose to manifest himself to the human species through Him in a special way. He taught us to be filled with the Holy Spirit of God's Love within our own souls, and to accept forgiveness and compassion for ourselves and for our fellow man. We too are connected to the God-Source of creation within our inner soul. We are ALL considered the sons and daughters of the Father/Mother universal nature of creation. Read (NKJV) 1st John 3: Verse 1> "Behold what manner of love the Father has bestowed on us, that we should be called children of God!" . . .

THE TRUE TEMPLE OF GOD IS
IN YOUR OWN SOUL . . . .

I have learned that the true temple of God is in your own soul body. Within the spiritual soul-core of your HEART, the etheric-purifying fire of the HOLY SPIRIT OF GOD RESIDES, once it is activated.

There is nothing wrong with going to a neighborhood church. I did so myself for many years. I also took my children to church when they were very young to help them form a foundation for the Love of God. I baptized them in the lake that I grew up on. Now that I am older I don't feel the need to go every week, yet I still go on an occasion to a Messianic Church service nearby my home. I have a good foundation and a spiritual relationship DIRECTLY with the God source of my soul. My tithing often goes to the homeless or to the man on the corner asking for a few dollars. Today, I would say that I am more spiritual than religious. I spend personal time with God in prayer and meditation in my own personal way, throughout my daily routine of living life to its fullest. I still attend church occasionally. Working every other weekend as a nurse is not always compliant to the hours of church services. My spiritual connection to God is more personal than public.

BEING BORN AGAIN . . . .

. . . . When I experienced my visionary near-death experience I was filled with the Holy Spirit of God. What I had experienced was being born again, not of the flesh, but of a spiritual nature. When I pray to the God-source, my prayers are answered when I pray "directly" to the Father. It is our soul that is made in the likeness of the true source of God, not our physical body. When we invite the spiritual light of Christ into our hearts, an awakening takes place within the deepest core center of our heart and soul. We actually feel lighter and free from within. Jesus taught us to follow the light of God; to make choices one step at a time, towards the light of the Holy Spirit filled with the nature of love. This pure love is from the heart of your soul, not the physical body. Jesus taught that the only way to the Father was through the Holy Spirit and the Christ consciousness of God. We too, can be filled with the Light of God the Father. Early Christianity describes the Holy Spirit as the divine Mother/ female aspect of God's Love to include the combination of the divine Father/male aspect. It's a balance between the two electro-magnetic forces of nature.

BE CAREFUL WHAT
YOU THINK . . . .

. . . . Protect you thoughts. Everyone has negative thoughts pop up into their mind and consciousness at times. I have trained my mind to say: "cancel, cancel", and to totally release these negative thoughts. I will immediately replace them with a positive thought or outcome. I even shed light on the situation in my own mind-mapping of thoughts to achieve a better outcome. It works! Try it. In the course of one day we can think about 1000 words or more. Guard your own self-talk. Think good thoughts about yourself. Often, we are the worst critics of ourselves. Stop beating yourself up inside and think of what you want to become and make it happen, one day at a time. Remember, kind words go a long way to form a healthy heart.

I AM NOT A SAINT . . . .

. . . . Having an experience like this does not make one a saint. I have had the same struggles and lessons to learn as everyone else that this life has to offer. What I have learned is that each day is a new day. We learn from our mistakes and say to ourselves:

"Next time I will do a better job".

When I do make a poor choice in life, I have learned from that experience and try not to repeat the same mistake twice.

The sun always rises with an opportunity for new beginnings. We have a clean slate to try again to perfect ourselves each day. Our self-talk can be forgiving towards our own life and to others. We can learn how to be a forgiving person. That does not mean that we need to forget what has happened. We can forgive the sinner and still not accept or condone the sin or transgression that may have transpired. When we come to God and ask for forgiveness, who are we to hold a grudge towards someone else? To receive forgiveness from our Loving Father-Mother God, places us in a position to be more forgiving to our fellow man. We become more patient towards others. It doesn't mean that we let others walk all over us either. We have the right to speak our truth, or to just walk away. Sometimes we will have to agree to disagree on certain subjects.

Some of us take longer to learn the same lesson over and over until we get it right. It may take more than one life in my opinion.

Time heals all things I have learned. Being patient with ourselves and others is a key to a happy life. I have experienced relationships of Love, friendship, betrayal, anger, disappointment, and forgiveness. Some of our worse experiences are those within our own families. Some of them may be at school or in the workplace. I have learned that the storms of life always settle to a perfect calm until the next challenge arises. This too will pass and we become a stronger person. We also learn to speak up for ourselves when a situation needs to be changed for the better. We learn to set boundaries with some relationships and surround ourselves with a circle of loving relationships that are healthy.

Through the years I have asked the Holy Spirit of God to send me the right people in my life to get me through certain hardships. It's okay to "ask" for help. I have learned that God won't always intervene unless we **ask for help** in our own private prayers.

> (NKJV) Mathew 7: Verse 7> "**Ask,** and it will be given to you; **seek,** and you will find; **knock,** and it will be opened to you."
>
> Verse 8> "For everyone who asks receives, and he who seeks finds, and to him who knocks it will be opened".
>
> (NKJV) John 14: Verse 13> "And whatever you ask in My name, that I will do, that the Father may be glorified in the Son".
>
> Verse 14> "If you ask anything in My [Jesus] name, I will do it. Vs 15> "If you love Me, keep My

commandments. Vs 16> "And I will pray the Father, and He will give you another **Helper**, that He may abide with you forever—Vs 17> "the Spirit of truth, whom the world cannot receive, because it neither sees Him nor knows Him; but you know Him, for He dwells with you and will be in you." Vs 26> "But the **Helper, the Holy Spirit,** whom the Father will send in my [Jesus] name, He will teach you all things, and bring to your remembrance all things that I said to you."

LESSONS OF LIFE IN ELEMENTARY SCHOOL; LIFE CAN BE HUMBLING . . . .

When I was in the first grade the bridge of my nose was fractured and broken while playing outside on the hard cemented recess area. The recess bell rang that was an indication to let us know that it was time to go back into the building. I remember a large mass of children running towards me as we all turned to approach the entrance to the building. Somehow, someone mistakenly tripped me and I was trampled by the massive group of children running back into the school. It happened so fast that I could not reach out with my hands to soften my fall. I landed head first with a direct face plant into the rocky hard surface. My shoulders and arms lay straight down by my sides. I pushed myself up after the onslaught of children passed me by. Not one child stopped to help me. I looked around to see if there was an adult nearby, but they too were gone from the area. I slowly walked into the building holding my painful nose. I then approached the teacher as I entered the classroom and asked her if I could go see the nurse. She just scolded me and said that I was making up a story to get out of school. I was instructed to go back to my chair in the back of the classroom. I was too shy to stand up to her so I slowly went back to my desk. I'll never forget that first grade teacher. She was one of the meanest people I had ever known in my life up to that time. I didn't learn much from her as a result. Due to my face plant into the hard rock surface of the recess play area, I formed a big bump on the bridge of my nose. This bump has stayed with me all of my life. Later on in my life as an adult, an x-ray was taken that proved a fracture line break on each side of my nose. From that day forward, there was often a child that would ask me why I had such a big nose. It wasn't so bad that my mother thought it necessary to take me to the Doctor. Yet it did present me with a humbling experience that has stayed with me all of my life, as plain as day, as the nose on my face! I must say, as I grew older it wasn't as bad as I once thought, but it did keep me humble and more sensitive to others that were less than perfect. I learned to view people for who they were as a person, not just what they looked like on the outside. Physical imperfections are only skin deep. It's who you really are on the inside of your soul that is the most important. We are more than just our physical bodies.

EARNING RESPECT . . . .

. . . . My first grade teacher that I just referred to was my first experience of being treated less than respectful. She was quite old with gray hair and looked exactly like the picture of the old lady in my old-maid playing deck of cards. I remember telling my sister this as we played the game. She didn't believe me until one day she actually met her. She then agreed that yes, she was a perfect resemblance. The common saying that: "You have to earn my respect", is often true. Yet it does not mean that we treat the very young with disrespect. My teacher, would speak civil to the parents, but often speak rude to the children when there were no other adults around. I learned to tune her out and became a perfect day dreamer.

My second grade teacher was also a white haired woman. She had a slightly better disposition. However, if you spoke during class she would snap your hand with a wooden ruler. I got hit only once by that swift snap of a ruler. She used it like a fly swatter. We learned quite quickly to "sit up straight" and "keep our mouths shut". Those first few years of elementary school are so important on how we treat our children. It can make or break a very young child's tender ego. I didn't have a nice or cheerful teacher until I reached sixth grade. Somehow I survived my younger years of schooling. When I became a parent later in my life, I learned to become an advocate for my own children as they grew up. Fortunately, my children had better teachers that treated them with much more respect. The laws have now been changed for the better so that it is against the law to hit a child.

Thank God for the parents who sought out for better laws to make school a safe and pleasant experience for our youth. As a result of my own experiences, one of my mottos is:

> "Children learn to treat others with respect by being treated with respect themselves".

NEITHER A LEADER OR A FOLLOWER . . . .

As a young teenager I was not a leader, but I didn't follow the crowd either. I remember a couple of my summer friends at the lake stealing away a cigarette from their parents stash. They huddled around the cigarette on the side of the house taking turns smoking it. When they offered it to me I said: "No". They made fun of me and called me: "Goody two shoes". I remember just walking away to go home without saying anything in return to defend myself. I silently and quietly slipped away. The next day I went back to play with them again and they asked me why I didn't take a smoke. I told them that I wasn't interested because my father had been a chain smoker when I was younger. I had to put up with his secondary smoke in the back seat of the car when he was driving. I use to beg him to stop smoking in the car when I was little. It was very unpleasant.

Don't get me wrong. Many of my good friends smoke, and I am not making a judgment that it is wrong. Even though my father smoked when I was a very small child; he was still a very good person. However, he thankfully quit as he got older and was smoke free for many years. There's an old saying that explains that it's best when taking everything in moderation but not in excess. When a substance takes hold of one's life and becomes an addiction, this is when it is not a healthy practice.

My main point is to say: It is okay to say: "NO", if you don't want to follow the crowd.

Later in middle school, we had been requested to write a story on what we had done while on summer break.

I explained while on vacation, I had visited the zoo with my cousins. As we toured the petting zoo, I saw a child dart in front of me like a rolling ball on the ground. This very young child had no arms and no legs; only stubs where the limbs should have been. To my astonishment this beautiful child had a smile that shined from ear to ear, so I offered my own smile in return.

When back in school later that year, with my assignment in hand, I did a personal search in the library. I learned that some physical anomalies or birth defects can be caused by genetic familial traits of the unborn child while forming in the womb; others can be caused by certain medications or recreational drugs that were taken during one's pregnancy.

I knew that I wanted to have healthy children in my life time if at all possible. The knowledge I obtained cured me from ever wanting to try recreational or harmful drugs for an entire lifetime.

I submitted a report on recreational drugs, and the affects they have on the unborn child. My report explained some of these major side effects are known to cause abnormalities in your ovaries; producing an infant to have serious birth defects even years after you had previously ingested them. Needless to say, I got an A+ on my report that year in middle school.

It's better to say: "NO!" to harmful recreational drugs. They often lead you down a darkened road to a sad end. Remember, **do not be a weak minded follower even if some of your best friends are becoming users.**

Just simply walk away and surround yourself with healthier people and a circle of friends who make healthy choices in life.

There's always a way out to create a better life. However, it's better never to start, because sometimes it's harder to stop addictions when trying certain substances only once. **Be strong** within your own being, **simply walk away**, and **say no to recreational and harmful drugs**!

GROWING UP IN HIGH SCHOOL . . . .

I was never a very good student when I was younger. It was not until my near-death vision that I began to see the world with a different perspective. Before, as a younger child I was a day-dreamer and did not pay attention in school; totally disinterested. My elementary school years were not pleasant to me as I have previously described. Somehow I got by, and passed every year to the next grade. However, when I started to pay attention, my grades shot up to the honor roll.

I became very active in band and dance drill team. Our school had a very small populous due to the surrounding country setting. There were only about 250 children in my High School. Almost 200 of us were in the band and drill team. In my sophomore year, we were fortunate enough to be invited to be in the Rose Bowl parade in Pasadena, California for the New Year's Day of 1970. That was a complete treat for most of us since it was our first time in an airplane let alone going on a trip without our parents. As we approached California from the air, I couldn't believe how many people actually had swimming pools in their back yards! It didn't dawn on me at the time that I was the luckier one to actually have a lake for my front yard. We stayed at the UCLA College dorms and had three buses to drive us around to our destinations. One of which was Disney Land and Marine Land. We had a wonderful time.

I especially remember one of our bus driver's was a pretty big guy about 300 lbs. One of our classmates gave him the nick name of "twiggy" so that name stuck for him from that day on. Twiggy at the time, was a famous model who had a slender and almost anorexic appearance. We were later told that we were the nicest group of kids that the bus drivers had ever worked with. They later flew up to our school to visit. One of them planned to relocate and move to the area just because we had made such a good impression.

Speaking of buses, most of the land between the school and my home at the lake was farm land. I actually lived the farthest away from my school than most of my friends. I was the first one on the bus and the last to go home. It took me an hour on the bus each morning and another hour to get home. When I got off of the bus, I had another mile before I arrived home. If it was a nice day I would walk home. But most of the time I was lucky enough to have a ride home in the car. My devoted mother would be sitting there waiting for us to arrive if the weather was not so appealing. I did the same for my children even though the bus was only two blocks away from our home. If it was raining or snowing they got a ride in the car in the early mornings. I would even heat up the car prior to getting into it, so it was nice and toasty warm.

My mother was a good role model. When I was very small I recall being frightened by the loud strikes of thunder above our lake home. She assured me that there was nothing to be scared of and that it was actually quite beautiful to look at from inside of the house. She then turned off all of the lights and had me look outside the front picture window of our home. When the lightning struck, it would light up the entire lake as the fingers of electrical shafts of electricity streaked across the dark sky above. It was really quite beautiful! From that night on, I was never afraid of thunder or lightening. In fact I loved the sound of the rain drops on the roof of our home because it was an aluminum roof. Due to the heavy snow falls, most homes in the area had an aluminum roof so the snow would easily slide off in the winter. The aluminum created a nice sound when the heavy rains would cause a down pouring over our home. I didn't mind the rain at all, as it created the comforting sounds of the pelting rainfall.

LATER IN LIFE AS A YOUNG ADULT . . . .

So my younger carefree days were a complete blessing. I lived a charmed life but didn't realize it when I was much younger. I was young and dumb and moved about 400 miles from the lake that I referred to as "Heaven of Earth". I wanted to find my way into the world, so I moved to the city. I attended a local college, and then moved to a larger metropolis to make my mark in the world of medical professionalism. Being a mother/baby nurse has served me well, and helped me find proper employment all my life. I have worked both in a hospital setting and as a nurse in a doctor's office. When my children were growing up, I worked in the clinic so I could have weekends and holidays off. It was a perfect situation to raise a family.

LESSONS OF LIFE IN THE WORK PLACE . . . .

In order to be home with my children on the weekends, I had secured a new job in an OB/GYN's Doctor's office. It was my second day working for this particular female Doctor. She was quite tired and cranky from working on call the night before. She was also training a new medical student that day which is quite draining to be a preceptor for someone new. I hardly knew this Doctor but I was performing my job without any problems. As I was standing behind the nurse's desk to assist her, she approached the desk to do some charting. This was before we were doing electronic charting on the computers. All the patients had a paper chart that had to be filled out by hand writing. I remember her looking up to me and making a rather rude disrespectful comment directly to me. She then looked at the medical student standing next to her then back to me, and said: "What are you going to say about that?" The medical student looked at me with a sheepish grin on her face to see how I was going to respond. I then looked back at the Doctor and lovingly said,

> "I have wide shoulders, a duck's back, and a warm heart".
> To be followed by, "Are you having a bad day Doctor, what can I do to help you?"

It was like my guardian angel was sitting on my shoulder giving me the words to say. The phrase of words just magically came out of nowhere and slid right off my tongue. I was just as surprised as the doctor seemed to be. The doctor ignored me and just continued with her charting as if I wasn't there. But I never had another problem with her from that day forward. In fact she apologized to me the following day, explaining that she had been on call the day before. We have actually become very good friends since that day. After working there for almost ten years while my children were growing up, I left and sought out a job in a near-by hospital. The Doctor's office was a wonderful place to work, with weekends and holidays off. It suited my life style at the time for the needs of my family at home. But now that my children are grown, I am back in the hospital working in a birth center again. When I was first married I also worked in Labor and Delivery in the hospital. This is where my passion is to help bring new life into the world.

WORK PLACE PROTOCOL.

I have also learned that not everyone will like everything about my personality, nor I theirs. I don't have a need to be liked by everyone. I will sometimes find a commonality that we both may have, and talk about that. I will avoid certain subjects that I don't agree with. There are times that you may have to agree to disagree if you feel the need to speak your own truth. Yet it is very important to speak to everyone with respect, especially in a professional work place. You don't have to be best friends with everyone you work with or go to school with. But it is very important to be kind to one another and be respectful. Leave your differences at the door when you enter the building. Keep your mind on your work and do the very best job that you have been hired to do. Take pride in your work and do it well. Have a friendly smile on your face and be a cheerful person. Leave your problems at home and keep them separate from the rest of the world. Only confide in a few close people that you may trust. If you wish to keep something secret at work, then don't tell anyone. If you tell one person, most likely the world of people around you will eventually know. It's best to keep your personal life and your work life somewhat separate.

SPIRITUAL AWAKENINGS/
KNUNDILINI ENERGY

Before I met my husband, I was a fundamental Christian. I had read my bible inside and out. I thought that I knew everything that I needed to know about spiritual matters. I was about to find out differently as I will explain. My self-righteous demeanor was about to be pulled out beneath my feet. God has a way of humbling us when needed.

When I was first married, I had gone to a Physician who specialized in back surgery. I had injured the lower lumbar area of my back in my earlier years due to gymnastics while in High School. He gave me the diagnosis of "degenerative disk disease." He told me that I was a candidate for surgery, but that he could not guarantee that it would make my back any better. In fact the surgery could make the problem worse. I thanked him for his honesty and decided against having surgery at all. Instead, I turned to alternative medicine. My mother-in-law took me to a spiritual Reiki healer. I had heard of therapeutic touch for healing because some hospitals still use this practice. I was ready to try anything that might help. The healing is provided from the energy of the practitioner by placing their hands over and above the soft tissue or skin of the affected pain. They then provide their own healing energy towards your body with the energy from their hands. With this practice, they combine their intent of healing thoughts. I entered the office of the Reiki healer. When my name was called, I was led to a private room that had a long cushioned healing table to lie down on. He had me lay down on my back. I was comforted by soft music and the aroma of incense. I felt safe and at ease. I did not really expect any major healing, but I was willing to try anything. My mother-in-law recommended this particular practitioner. As the Reiki healer walked around the healing table he asked me to take a few deep breaths. As I did so, I subconsciously thought: "Let's get this over with". I took another three deep breaths as I arched my back. By the third breath I spontaneously experienced what they call Knundalini energy. This phenomenon is an altered yet heightened state of consciousness. It can be activated not only by a near-death experience, or by accepting the Holy Spirit within your soul, but also by a certain practice of Yoga breathing.

It creates an inner transformation of self to the enhanced realization that we are truly a child of God within the universe. Your physical mind is expanded to a higher plane of thought. Some Yoga masters will train for this in meditation for years before finally experiencing what they call knundalini in the ancient texts.

Until this happened to me spontaneously, I had never heard of it, nor did I previously know that it even existed. Within my inner intuitive eye I could see the anatomy of my own auric field that resided around my physical body, sometimes called bio-rhythms. At the base of one's spine in the sacral space of our endocrine system lies an energy source that lies dormant until activated. When our inner soul is matured to a certain gestation, this energy source is spontaneously released. It then travels upward to the pituitary and pineal glands in the auric field where they reside in the crown of our head. When this occurs, an awakening takes place that brings your physical mind's awareness in unison with your soul memory. There is a blending of the two. It's like waking up from night to day. Within this new found spiritual awakening I could see the spiritual light around my body which is called our "Aura". In my [mind's eye] or what is referred to your third eye, (in alignment with the pineal gland within our endocrine system), I could actually see my aura! It only lasted for several minutes, but it made an impression upon my senses. Afterwards, I began to remember my soul memory of the past life I had when in Paris. I began to read books on the anatomy of one's soul. The pictures I saw in the ancient texts matched that which I had literally seen in my own personal experience.

When the light of Father-Mother God's love bursts forth within ones soul; it does so like a flower of the universe unfolding in full array. Our soul literally is part of the essence & nature of Gods universe. Our heart sings with the vibration of His-Her Love. It is an extension of the Holy-Spirit.

From what I have read in other literature; the light of Christ that surges forth is also called pranic breath in yoga meditation practices, "Enso" or endless light to the student of the Jewish Kabbalist; or "primal vibration" in ancient teachings. In biblical terms it is referred to as "Logos" or the "Word of God".

This spiritual light liberates your inner soul being from darkness, replacing it with the light of the universe. When this occurs, your soul is dressed in the white robes of etheric white light of pure blissful Love from the source of God. For that brief moment, I felt one with God within my soul. This higher vibration is transcendent, above physical matter. Keeping this higher vibration is not always easy; however, I believe that Jesus had mastered this level of divine vibration within his own soul body and maintained it.

The meaning of the word Christ means: "The anointed one". He truly was the Christ of God who walked the earth within his own soul.

THE FRUITS OF THE
HOLY SPIRIT . . . .

Some of these fruits are:

Being filled with the Love and Light of Christ, Being One with Creation within your inner soul, knowledge of the invisible mysteries that bring about eternal change, Loving kindness, truth, freedom, joy, peace, harmony, wisdom, insight, perception, spiritual understanding, perfection, soul memories, thoughtfulness, grace, forethought, fore-knowledge, Life eternal, charity, good works, to create and preserve that which is beautiful, self-discipline, to seek the cycles of existence within the laws of nature and Creation, to become alive in Christ.

FRUITS OF THE CARNAL FLESH . . . .

Some of these fruits are:

Being imprisoned in spiritual darkness, arrogance, ignorance of spiritual knowledge, overly critical, self-righteousness, false pride, sin, hatred, jealousy, unholy desires, lust, sacrilege, corrupt, confinement, greed, self-gratification, gluttony, self-serving, stealing, unrighteous anger, contempt, rebellion, giving in to the lower instincts of the temptations of our carnal flesh, to make war with others, dead in Christ.

LIFE CONTINUES . . . .

My physical spine seemed to be healed from the energy I had experienced during the Reiki session. I still had to be careful with certain physical activities, but I could now live with my back pain with less discomfort. I took calcium to help my back grow stronger for a better bone density of strength. As a result of experiencing this spiritual awakening, I began to question my fundamental teachings; especially when I could access my soul's memory of reincarnation. At the end of my book will be a page of recommended reading. One of those books will be by Jim B Tucker, M.D. that is a study of children's memories of previous lives.

After years of much study, I realize that the bible is compiled of spiritually inspired words of truth, yet not all of the inspired works were included in the bible as we know it. From what I have read, some of the early Church fathers of Christianity did believe in reincarnation. When we start researching the teachings of early Gnostic Christians gospels, they will enlighten your awareness of the deeper mysteries that were once taught long ago. When you study the history of Roman rule you will discover that they chose not to include the teachings of reincarnation or karma when they selectively put together the New Testament of the Bible as we know it today.

History tells us that during the fifth century A.D. the Roman emperor Justinian sanctioned the Church to eradicate the teachings of reincarnation, karma, and compassion. Those who did not adhere to these new laws were labeled heretics.

The powers of Rome's politically controlled Church were very selective in compiling the books that made up the New Testament of the bible as we know it today. However, there were several other gospels that were left out.

I recommend a book called: "Forbidden Faith", "the Gnostic Legacy", by Richard Smoley. I recommend it for further reading of the history of the Catholic Church and how it has formulated to its present day.

Rome's well groomed Church of political unrest fashioned a plan to exclude reincarnation all together. Their aim was to demand total submission to the governing laws of state and Church. Molding their public servants of their jurisdiction into complete conform under their ruling thumb which was governed by the Emperor by Justinian.

Since my travels concerning the quest for complete truth, I have become much more open minded. I still accept the manifestation of Christ and the Love of the Holy Spirit within the Divinity of Jesus Christ; He truly embodied the living God who walked the earth. I embrace his teachings with fuller understanding. We too can follow his example and be a conduit of Christ's love. It is the Christ consciousness that Jesus embodies that we embrace. The word Christ means, 'The anointed One'; the anointing of the Holy Spirit of Creation.

The truth of Gods revelations do not end from years past. God continues to reach out to those who seek him on a present day basis from all over the world and from many different cultures in a spiritual way.

UNITY CONSCIOUSNESS . . . .

. . . . Unity consciousness is knowing who you really are within your soul. When we first come into the human body, we take on the physicality of forgetfulness. Our human brain has no memory of a pre-existence in the beginning of our journey in this third dimensional life. As our physical body grows into a young child we sometimes begin to have soul memories. They can take form in the revelation of a dream that may reoccur time and time again. When our soul begins to experience a spiritual awakening, we realize that the universe is a vast consciousness, teaming with life; we then see that we truly are a tiny seed of this vastness. The spiritual awakening of the knundalini rising within the anatomy of our soul helps us to comprehend that we are only a microcosm within the macrocosm of this universe. This experience transcends the limits of the human mind. Within the heart center of our soul is the portion that is sometimes referred to as the star seed. We all are actually connected to the God Source within our inner being. Once our physical body grows, the auric field of our etheric soul body can completely blend like an over soul within our physical body. The next step is to invite the baptism of the holy spirit of God which is the cosmic etheric Christ into our hearts. Once we accept this mantel of cleansing power and love from the Father of the Universe sometimes referred to as the God source; we are connected to what is called Unity consciousness. The baptism I speak of is not the baptism of your outer physical body with an emersion of water. Though, this practice symbolizes the inner baptism of the soul within. Water baptism is not necessary to experience the baptism of the Holy Spirit inside your soul. I experienced the inner mantel of baptism of God's illuminating cleansing power, first. The water baptism is just a formality and a symbol of the deeper mysteries of the Holy Spirit. From what I have read, it takes an infant up to twelve years to mature physically, in order to house the entirety of our soul's anatomy. As I understand this process, the endocrine glands of our physical body serve as the storehouse of vibrational energy. Just like the working of a well-greased car, our human body is powered by several working parts that work together as a whole. The endocrine glands in particular have unique properties that contribute to our complete health. Yet their functions are not confined to the physical working of our whole self-portrait. Within them is a vortex of energy that radiates outward in a wheel of vibrational bio-rhythms. They collectively serve as a matrix of energy that forms around and within our body. Just as the earth has a north-pole and a south-pole with a pillar of electro-magnetic energy field within, it also serves as a protective force field of energy, ... we too have what we call a bio-rhythm of energy that runs from the crown of our head to the base of our spine in the sacrum, creating a pillar of lighted energy within and around our bodies. Our souls blend with this energy field creating an over soul around our body, sometimes called a "Merkabah". "MER" means: "Light", "KA" means: "Spirit", "BA": means: "Body". Our souls actually pre-existed before blending with the human body. Have you ever noticed the "glow" of a pregnant woman? This light emanation that hovers around the mother's physical body before birth is the soul of the fetus.

Our soul actually attaches itself within the auric field of the mother to be; this attachment resembles an umbilical cord, yet it is comprised of etheric energy in nature, as is your soul. Another name for this tethered cord is referred to as the silver cord of attachment. Once the infant grows into a young child approximately around the age of twelve, our soul body can completely connect to the human body via the endocrine glands. It's like each endocrine gland is a power point of energy. I picture our soul like an etheric overcoat that buttons into place at the center of each endocrine gland. We each house a mantel of energy signature around and within our bodies forming the anatomy of our soul. Our soul is etheric, not physical. Like a radio wave of energy. It has its own vibrational signature. Have you ever been in an elevator with complete strangers, yet felt their energy pattern? This vibration of energy is unique to everyone.

I have actually met certain people who can see auras with their physical eyesight most all of their lives. But most of us do not have that sixth sense as they fortunately do. The etheric workings of our soul's anatomy are referred to what they call: "Chakras" by ancient teachings. A chakra is a spherical energy-vortex or wheel of energy emitting from each endocrine gland within our bodies. Our soul in comprised of seven major chakras that line up with the seven major endocrine glands in our physical body. These **CHAKRAS** are what I will refer to as **SPHERICAL LIFE CENTERS.**

The 1st Life-Center > Root Chakra > Coccygeal gland
The 2nd Life-Center > Spleen Chakra > Splenic gland
The 3rd Life-Center > Navel Chakra > Thoracic gland
The 4th Life-Center > Heart Chakra > Cardiac gland
The 5th Life-Center > Throat Chakra > Pharyngeal gland
The 6th Life-Center > Brow Chakra > Pituitary gland
The 7th Life-Center > Crown Chakra > Pineal gland

Within these life centers, the yin/yang energy resides. The Yin/Yang symbol is a symbol that depicts the female/male energies as a whole. It symbolizes the "balance" of both parties.

It reflects the same energy of a battery with the negative and positive charge. Together they form a complete unit of autonomic electro-magnetic charge.

When I first studied the symbol of yin/yang I was personally offended; because the dark side explains that the female is negative. And the white side portrays that the male as positive. I could not comprehend why the female would be thought of as negative. I took the words literally instead of symbolically. Then after studying it much further, I realized that this ancient symbol is the alchemy of a battery. The negative/female side is magnetic, while the positive/male side is electric. When you blend these two parties together what do you get? An ASCENSION of power within! How simple is that! These two properties dwell within our own personal soul's anatomy. **The yin/yang symbol is the balance of the electro-magnetic properties in the bio-rhythms of one's soul.**

So what is Ascension and the purpose for it? When Ascension takes place, the Cosmic Christ energy can then dwell in its purest form of etheric light within the orb of one's soul. Once a spiritual seeking student completely embodies the fullness of God's light within the entirety of body mind and soul, the Resurrection takes place after death. The Ascension is the alchemy of light within one's soul body. The Resurrection is the complete embodiment of light within one's physical body; the release from the Dragon's ego within. Jesus taught us to FOLLOW HIM, for we too can move mountains.

I do believe that God has sent many teachers to mankind, to enlighten our spiritual understandings. I personally have discovered that there is truth in other spiritual teachings around the world other than Christian literature. God has no barriers in reaching out to the human race from all different cultures and belief systems.

Yet I believe that Jesus was completely aware of his soul memories at a very young age and was a conduit of the divine will of the God Source. The bible explains that when he was only twelve years of age, that he was in the temple tending to his Father's business.

According to some literature that I have read, that he became a priest in the order of Melchizedek. Of whom I speak, is mentioned in the Old Testament. It has been said in Jewish literature, that the Messiah would come from the order of Melchizedek.

I recommend these scriptures in the bible for those who wish to study more information about Melchizedek and His role in biblical history:

(NKJV): Genesis 14:18, Psalms 110:4, Hebrews 5: 6-10. Hebrews 7: 11-17:

(NKJV): Hebrews 7: Verse 21 > "(for they have become priests without an oath, but He with an oath by Him who said to Him:

"The Lord has sworn

And will not relent,

'You are a priest forever

According to the order of

Melchizedek'"),

Verse 22: > "by so much more Jesus has become a surety of a better covenant."

Verse 26:> "For such a High Priest was fitting for us, who is holy, harmless, undefiled, separate from sinners, and has become higher than the heavens;"

Verse 27: > "who does not need daily, as those high priests, to offer up sacrifices, first for His own sins and then for the people's, for this He did once for all when He offered up Himself."

He fulfilled his predestined purpose for coming into this world as a teacher of God's Word by the age of 30. Did he actively perfect his soul to embody and MAINTAIN the LIGHT and the ANOINTING OF CHRIST; then house the divinity of the Father/God-source of the universe which expels all darkness within? **His soul was in pre-existence** before he came to this world. He knew his life's purpose from a very young age. He was pre-destined to accomplish this very goal. The Messiah has come to lead us to the 'second birth', the birth of our soul.

(NKJV): Hebrews 9: Verse 11> "But Christ came as High Priest of the good things to come, with the greater and more perfect tabernacle not made with hands, that is, not of this creation."

Verse 12> "Not with the blood of goats and calves, but with His own blood He entered the Most Holy Place once for all, having obtained eternal redemption."

Verse 15> "And for this reason He is the Mediator of the new covenant, by means of death, for the redemption of the transgressions under the first covenant, that those who are called may receive the promise of the eternal inheritance."

WHEN THE STUDENT IS READY, THE TEACHER WILL APPEAR . . . .

The sacred mysteries of Holy Spirit are hidden and lay dormant. When the student is ready, the teacher will appear. You are ready, when your heart starts seeking answers.

All you need to do is to ask. Ask Jesus to show you the way.

It takes a life time to learn the layers of revelations that God places before us. It's an ongoing journey. The most-high God of LIGHT and LOVE will place before your journey, coincidences of spiritual awakenings as gifts to your soul along the path. When you are thirsty for truth within the deepest yearnings of your heart, the answers will come. Look and listen to the promptings of your higher self. Your super consciousness will guide you to the corridors of truth. Doors once closed will now be opened to the spiritual seeker who is hungry and thirsty for the higher revelations of the LIGHT from the God Source of our universe. The LIGHT that I speak of is not one of deception, but of the purest and most SACRED LIGHT benevolent to man, and for the highest good of your soul's evolution. Follow the teacher into the corridor to the central core chamber of the three fold flame within your heart chakra; there the Holy Spirit of LIGHT will guide you to the purest God source of LOVE. This force is very real and very powerful. I know, because I have felt the power of its presence within mine own soul. There really are no human words to explain it or describe it to the depth of its totality. The world of physical manifestation cannot comprehend it.

THE AURIC FIELD . . . .

Dr. Hiroshi Motoyama created the California Institute for Human Science. He has studied to become a Shinto priest, but also a scientist. Within his scientific studies I have read that he measured the energy levels of many students before and after meditation practices. This auric living energy field that resides within and around our physical body can also be captured on film with the science of Kirlian photography. This auric field of energy shows the light anatomy of our soul. I have actually had my personal photo taken in this fashion at a nearby spiritual book store. It showed the luminescence light emanating around my body. Different colors were present like the colors of a rainbow showing the refractions of light.

ONE GOD WITHIN THE
UNITY OF CREATION . . . .

I am aware that there are other religions besides fundamental Christianity who believe that there is only One God.

I also am aware that some people believe that Jesus was only a prophet. I believe different; He was also anointed the Christ.

Bible Verse: (NKJV): Acts 2: Verse 30 > "Therefore, being a prophet, and knowing that God had sworn with an oath to him that of the fruit of his body, according to the flesh, He would raise up throne,"

> Verse 31 > "he, foreseeing this, spoke concerning the resurrection of the Christ, that His soul was not left in Hades, nor did His flesh see corruption."
>
> Verse 32 > "This Jesus God has raised up of which we are all witnesses."
>
> Verse 33 > "Therefore being exalted to the right hand of the Father the promise of the Holy Spirit, He poured out this which you now see and hear."
>
> Verse 36 > "Therefore let all the house of Israel know assuredly that God has made this Jesus, whom you crucified, both Lord and Christ."
>
> Verse 38 > "Then Peter said to them, "Repent, and let every one of you be baptized in the name of Jesus Christ for the remission of sins; and you shall receive the gift of the Holy Spirit."

Verse 39 > "For the promise is to you and to your children, and to all who are afar off, as many as the Lord our God will call."

What todays Christians call the Holy Spirit is actually the energy of pure love and light, only found in creation from the source we call God. Our soul and physical body constitute a blending of two separate parts that combine to make a unity of ONE within the Laws of Creation.

According to some ancient Gnostic teachings that I have read, there is only Unity of the ONE TRUE SOURCE OF CREATION within our Universe. So when our soul is immersed in the Light of God's Love, our soul body or aura becomes ONE within the Unity of Creation. This is what I have personally experienced.

When I was a young girl at the age of fifteen, I received an answer from God concerning my questionings of what the Holy Spirit actually was. The answer I received was being enveloped within the purity of God's unconditional Love. So yes, I do believe in the Holy Spirit. I believe it's the energy of God's Love. I received the alchemy of God's Unconditional Love at soul level, believe me, it is a very powerful life-giving force.

The bible speaks of the promised Holy Spirit pouring out, first to Jesus; then to his disciples and to those who accepted his teachings.

I wish to repeat this scripture for good reason:

(NKJV): Acts 2: Verse 33> "Therefore being exalted to the right hand of God, and having received from the Father the promise of the Holy spirit, He poured out this which you now see and hear."

The purifying Holy Spirit also referred to as the fire of the Holy Spirit, not only cleanses but burns away all that is impure and dark within our soul. It is pleasant but very powerful.

Jesus was and is the embodiment of the cosmic Christ's energy. In some of the near-death experiences that I have read, some people have come back to say that they have actually met and seen Jesus. They marveled that His soul body outshined every other in the heavenly realm that they were shown. There are others who have taught that when we receive the baptism of the Holy Spirit and the forgiveness of sins, that the cycle of reincarnation is broken.

However, I do believe that it takes more than one lifetime to "personally" learn the lessons of soul maturity and loving kindness in the course of eternity.

Some suggest that we **choose** to come back to perfect our souls as we re-enter the school called Earth. There are many facets to form a diamond. I picture each incarnation one more facet of the whole within the evolution of times keeping.

In other literature from near-death experiences that I have read, some have learned that we come to this earth plain to learn individual consciousness; to gain spiritual knowledge from one life to the next until our soul matures.

Our soul is part of nature. It experiences the same cycles of growth much as the seasons of nature does with the four major seasons of spring, summer, fall, and winter. Yet this process is referred to in some of the ancient texts as the "transmigration of souls". I call them the seasons of the soul. These cycles cross over from this side of the veil then back again for a rest in-between lives in the etheric kingdom of the soul; a dimension beyond matter and the physical life. When we cross over at the end of our life and return to the world of spirit, our full soul consciousness returns and we remember who we are. We are more than just our physical bodies.

The wild lilies of the field, to include all perennial growth, return year after year. Yet each year they go through the process of rebirth in the spring as they die out towards the autumn and winter months, only to return again and again.

HISTORY OF THE CHRISTIAN CHURCH . . . .

As I have described before, in the year 553 AD the foundations of the Christian Church were radically changed to fit the wills of political powers of that time. The Gnostic Christians were silenced and later accused of being heretics. Some, but not all of the fundamental teachings were distorted and manipulated to serve the political agendas of the Church in power at that time. The ignorance of these political parties expelled the teachings of transmigration of souls, which taught the steps of evolution within, leading its followers to Ascension into the LIGHT of pure LOVE. This council also expelled the female component of the Godhead. The words, (The mother of the universe), were not placed in any of the sacred teachings of the New Testament which they compiled together. Valuable scriptures were left out. Only the "Father" of the Godhead was included in the books that they used to achieve their controlled bitter end. But now, we have much that was once silenced and thought to be forgotten. Many of the original gospels of the very first disciples of Jesus Christ are now available in the Nag Hammadi Library. Within these original sacred teachings are numerous Gnostic writings of sacred scriptures. One such writing especially catches my attention even more than some of the others, called: "The Sophia of Jesus Christ". Within the pages of these sacred teachings are the words, (The Mother of the Universe), and (The Father of the Universe). Both genders are equally honored and respected within the Godhead. The female component was not distorted or omitted in the original teachings of our Gnostic Christian disciples. To give honor to both our Sacred Mother and our Sacred Father was accepted. However, the bible does explain to honor thy mother and thy father, but it is suggestive of our earthy parents, not those of our souls. It's time to claim back our Mother God, as well as the Father God in the harmony of the Yin/Yang energy.

ANATOMY OF THE SOUL . . . .

When I saw my aura for the very first time, (the anatomy of my soul), I was not aware that it even existed! My spontaneous experience of the knundalini energy rising up my spine was a complete surprise. It placed me in a blissful-raptured state of heightened awareness that I did not know was possible. I equally felt both the Mother/Father God energy that they speak of in the ancient texts. What I saw was a very large etheric soft pink lotus flower, in full bloom. My aura had a glow of luminescence. I seemed to be incased within a cocoon of white light. The Reiki healer that was circling the healing table stood back in surprised awe as I laid there. He then said out loud, "You are so beautiful"! He had on special glasses that allowed him to see the refractions of luminous light. I lay there is total bliss within the oneness of God's energy. My physical mind was now blended with my soul; I found that I could access my soul memories for the very first time. It was an incredible experience! My spiritual world had now expanded to a greater awareness within the conscientious of universal creation that resides in nature. I began to read books on the anatomy of the soul. They described in pictorial detail exactly what I had seen within my own aura within the pages of books I was reading. I started to see pictures and statues of Buddha sitting on a lotus flower. At the time, I wondered why these truths were not included in the bible. Yet later, I would find out that there were hidden references to it in the book of Revelation.

After seeking out these deeper truths from ancient texts, It stretched my awareness and curiosity to the world of Eastern spirituality. My mind needed an explanation of what had happened. What I now know and comprehend is that our soul has seven major vortexes of energy flow called chakras. I call them "Life-Centers".

When they are in good repair and have a clear energy flow, the knundalini energy can be activated. It feels like a candle being lit from inside. This energy then travels up to each life center in almost a figure eight motion between the seven major chakras. As it does this, it entwines them in a braided motion back and forth up to the top crown chakra. Basically the light bulb of your inner soul has just been turned on in brilliant radiant light; along with it is a blissful state of sacred geometry within your own being. As I have explained previously, the kingdom of God is within you. When Jesus explained, "to know yourself", I believe He was speaking of the condition of the seven life centers within our body; to know and comprehend if there are any blockages. The ancient tradition of **Yoga breathing** is to help motivate the knundalini energy to become activated. Once this is accomplished, we are then immersed within this sacred flow of enlightenment of the female spirit of the Goddess energy along with the energy of the Father God's Source. It too is pure love with a sweetness beyond measure.

I wish to interject that it's very important to be anointed with the Holy Spirit BEFORE experiencing knundalini. It can be a very powerful transition in one's auric field. If it is not directed by the spirit of God, but by the force of one's will through forced meditation, great harm can come to the life centers of one's chakra system. It is also wise to be under the care of a trained Yogic practitioner, or Reiki healer. Yet I would still be very careful in choosing an instructor with this specific knowledge. If the Life-Centers are opened or activated before the natural evolution of time's keeping, one can be injured or suffer great physical trauma I have read. If the lower chakras are activated and the energy is directed downward instead of up, they can open the lower animal instincts of the individual. This may include their sexual drives and passions in an unholy directive; becoming slaves to their own physical passions. If one's soul is not ready, they awaken the ego of the carnal flesh. These four lower Life-Centers that are situated towards the base or root chakra are sometimes referred to as the "four beasts" in the book of Revelation. The heart Life-Center being one of them; if the heart has not awakened to that which is of a spiritual nature, then it turns towards the needs of the flesh only.

> (NKJV): Matthew 26: Verse 41 > "Watch and pray, lest you enter into temptation, The spirit indeed is willing, but the flesh is weak."

For me, it was purely a spiritual experience. I was much younger, and in and good physical condition. My heart and soul was already directed by the Holy Spirit.

It's not easy to contain this higher level of vibration for a lengthened time within the knundallini energy. Within this energy, one's soul is in direct union of the source of God. Yet, I believe Jesus was an adept at this type of meditation since he most likely studied the precepts of the Melchizedek order from the age of twelve to twenty nine. The ancient teachings of the Kabbalah speak of this spiritual awakening within one's soul. He started his public teachings around the age of thirty, when he chose his twelve disciples.

The bible explains that Jesus cleansed Mary Magdalene of seven devils. In our present century of understanding this has left many to wonder what this actually meant. Holes were left out of the original scriptures. I believe the true meaning was to help teach us the ways to cleanse the seven life centers, or seven seals within our inner soul, so that they will be able to support the knundalini rising into the Light. Everyone has these major seven chakras within their auric field. They just don't know it, because they cannot see it with their physical eyes.

In the bible, there is a reference to this second sight when Samson explains that he was blind but now he can see. He could actually see better in a spiritual way; this second sight can also be referred to as the 6th sense.

I actually know someone who has been able to see auras for most of her life. She told me she use to sit in the back of the classroom in elementary school and study her teacher's aura. She could not only see it, she learned how to read it and know what it meant. She too is a Christian and accepts reincarnation as fact.

Jesus also mentions in the bible, to Follow Him; that we too can move mountains.

> (KNJV) Matthew 17: Verse 20> "So Jesus said to them, "Because of your unbelief; for assuredly, I say to you, if you have faith as a mustard seed, you will say to this mountain, 'Move from here to there,' and it will move; and nothing will be impossible for you."
> Verse 21> "However, this kind does not go out except by prayer and fasting."
> (KNJV) 1st Corinthians 13: Verse 2> "And though I have the gift of prophesy, and understand all mysteries and all knowledge, and though I have all faith, so that I could remove mountains, but have not love, I am nothing."

(KJNV) Numbers 12: Verse 6 > "Then He said, "Hear now My words: If there is a prophet among you, I, the Lord, make Myself known to him in a vision; I speak to him in a dream.""

I accessed this information in a dream state. I was half awake, yet half asleep. I felt the power of the Holy Spirit anointing me while in this state of consciousness. It was explained to me that the word 'mountains' is being used as a symbol to explain the impurities and blockages within our soul body. When I fully awoke, I searched the internet's web of knowledge base for any information to confirm my vision. Yes, I found it in the Edgar Casey material! Edgar Casey was known to be a modern day prophet of his time; respected by many. The A.R.E. foundation was created to house all of the valuable information that was obtained during his lifetime.

He too had a visionary near death experience I have read. He was shown the SYMBOLIC meaning of the dream of John in the book of Revelation within the bible. He was shown the metaphoric and symbolic meanings that it entailed.

I wish to interject here that God does speak individually to his children in a direct way.

BIBLE VERSE: (NKJV): Act 2: Verse 17 > "And it shall come to pass in the last days, says God, That I will pour out of My Spirit on all flesh; Your sons and you daughters shall prophesy, Your young men shall see visions, Your old men shall dream dreams."

In my half-awake dream state, Jesus showed me that the word 'mountains', is being used as a metaphoric symbol that explain the blockages within our own life centers that the ancients called chakras, or seals. These mountains are symbolic to the portion of our soul that we have not allowed the Light of God to take hold. These mountains can also be viewed as temptations that we may still hold on to; those of which we have not given over to Christ; sometimes referred to as the plagues or temptations of the carnal flesh. As Jesus expressed in the bible, the spirit is willing but the flesh is weak.

I too fall short with my own struggles of life, becoming an emotional eater when stressful experiences occur, giving in to physical temptations. I also have struggled with what some call a sweet tooth. Too much sugar or caffeine in one's diet can also be addictive. We cannot put anyone on a pedestal because we all have shortcomings to overcome including myself. I am not better than anyone else; we are in this journey together.

The study and diagram of the Jewish Kabbalah explains this process of our ultimate ascension which leads us to reunite with the Light of God. It leads us to the three fold flame within the alchemy of pure conscious love and spiritual wisdom; it leads our inner body into the alchemy of the purifying fire of the Holy Spirit. It expels all darkness within our soul body. Our goal is to become filled with the light of Christ in body, mind, and soul.

When we first come into this present incarnation, our soul memory is incased in a forgetfulness of who we really are within our inner being. Our human brain and conscious mind does not have these memories until our hearts turn to the source of God; becoming a spiritual seeker. Some describe this as falling from the Grace of God; falling to a lower consciousness.

SYMBOLIC CHARACTER REFERENCES IN THE BIBLE . . . .

The bible is encoded with archetypal symbols which were understood by our Gnostic forefathers. These symbols or icons have double meanings that are described in human terms or stories. These parables are presented to help us comprehend their true meanings. The number seven is a sacred number. Holy scriptures describe these seven spherical life centers of our soul as the seven lamps, seven candlesticks, or seven stars. In the book of Revelation they are referred to as the seven seals, or seven churches. In today's science they are called the seven major endocrine glands. BEFORE we open our hearts to receive the Holy Spirit they are referred to as the seven devils, or the seven Kings. These (earthly Kings), represent the war lords of darkness. Our goal is to overcome darkness with light. These seven centers are literally in darkness, void of the light until they are activated with the spirit of God's LOVE.

ASCENSION>THE BRIDEGROOM AWAITS US . . . .

The Christ energy is likened to our bridegroom, which represents the Yang/male portion of the symbol of balance. At the base of our spine within the sacrum, is our first life center sometimes referred to the root chakra. This first center represents the Yin/female MAGNETIC energy of our being; likened to the south-pole. Within it, is a coiled energy pattern that lays dormant, until activated by the Light of Christ. When this happens, the coiled energy releases itself and travels upward towards the crown of our head. It crisscrosses between the spheres of light centers like the pattern of a braided rope. As this energy continues upward to the top chakra, it activates each life center as if it is turning on the light in a darkened room. When it reaches the sixth and seventh center within the crown of our head, it activates our intuitive "third" eye as the Christ energy is released. This fountain of energy then baths us in the cascading waters of white light from the cosmic Christ consciousness. Our inner soul is now dressed in a mantel of Light. Our soul and mind are in complete at-one-ment with God's energy of love and light. The seven life centers are now literally alive! The rivers of living energy can now flow within every aspect of our soul; literally transitioning us to be clothed in a spiritual mantel of pure white light within our inner being.

The bridegroom awaits us at the seventh life center. The bridegroom is another symbol of the Christ/Yang (male) energy.

He is calling us to dine with him. When this happens, the Christ energy is released within our soul. Lose yourself into his care and the bindings of the dragon's ego of lower animal instincts: (the lower four life centers) will be cleansed, casting out all darkness. These lower four chakras are the basic animal instincts within our physical body; sometimes referred to as the four beasts.

These lower life centers are magnetic in nature from the Yin (female) energy. The upper three life centers are electric in nature from the Yang (male) energy.

When these two energies of Yin/Yang merge into one, they are intertwined in what is referred to as, the dance of life. The powerful life force in our inner being dances with the song of Christ; we dine at his table with the nourishment of the highest super-consciousness of God's Love and Light. The Christ has risen within your own soul!

Basically, your inner battery has been plugged in. The electro-magnetic forces within your inner soul have been activated to cause ANCENSION of the life force which once stood dormant.

The temple of God now resides within our inner being. The table of living manna from God . . . . the chalice of sweet honey from the Father's etheric Love, drips down from head to toe, like a shower cascading within your inner being. In the bible it is referred to as the river of living waters. As it travels downward, it cleanses and purifies your inner being in a baptism of complete purity and bliss. The darkness has turned into light. For the first time, you are alive in Christ! This is what the bible calls the second birth.

As I have explained before, our bodies have a bio-rhythm of magnetic energy that resides at the base of our spine in the root life center. The Yin/Yang energy literally resembles a battery. Our crown life center has a bio-rhythm that serves as an electric pathway of energy within our brain function.

There are synapses in our brain that give off sparks of energy in our autonomic or sympathetic nervous systems. These nerve pathways lead to the five senses in our body. I have read that these are represented in the book of Revelation in the Bible as the 24 elders. The synapse or electrical spark of energy between brain pathways within our brain, functionally serves as an electrical response. (Together) with the Yin/female magnetic force that resides at the base of our spine, and the yang/male electric force that resides in our brain called the pineal gland, they form a type of electro-magnetic response within one's soul body when activated. This is what the Yoga masters call knundalini.

According to the visionary near-death experience Edgar Casey had, it was revealed to him that the story in Revelation of John's prophetic dream is also a metaphoric parable to describe the anatomy of our inner body and soul. Scientific terms were not known in ancient times to describe this inner anatomy that we accept in our present day's anatomy classes.

The seven seals are metaphoric symbols for the seven chakras which I refer to as seven major life centers within our own soul anatomy. The great war of the Armageddon also represents the war between good and evil or light and darkness within the temple of our own individual souls. This war that is spoken of in the bible is another archetypal symbol depicting the struggle between light and dark within our own body, mind, and soul. The rapture is depicted as the second coming of Christ; which is the rising of life energy I just described. This rising up is called by some, Knundalini in the eastern world. It's yet another form the ascension of the Holy Spirit; the 'second birth of the soul' within each one of us. I encourage each and every one of you to seek the spiritual path that leads you to the enlightenment of the Holy Spirit of the anointing of Christ's energy that Jesus taught us. Change your dark robes and put on the robes of light, for the Kingdom of God is within you!

There is only one path to the very top of the mountain. The path that leads us to the pinnacle of the pyramid is where the all seeing eye of God resides within the cap stone.

Many will start at different angles from the base of the pyramid or mountain, but the very pinnacle can only be approached in one way as you journey up to the top. This refers to the pineal and pituitary glands within the 6th and 7th chakras. You can see the image of this pyramid on the one dollar bill of the United States currency with the all seeing eye of the cap stone. This eye is also likened to the 'third eye' of our own soul anatomy. It is indicative of our intuitive spiritual eye that is comprised of what some call the 6th sense, transcendent beyond physical limitations and that of mater. One can actually see the aura of the soul that houses and surrounds one's whole person.

This path is depicted as the knundalini rising.

The ultimate goal of our inner soul is to be reunited with the Spirit of the Father God. Our human body is incased within the yin/female energy that has been separated from the yang/male energy. The story of Adam and Eve in the Garden of Eden is another story or parable of the fall of mankind. Eve, the yin/energy, separated herself from the grace of God. She partook of the fruit of good and evil. She separated her soul from the Light of Christ's energy. Our soul remains in the void of darkness until the spirit of God reunites us with the Light of the Holy Spirit.

THE STORY OF THE
LOTUS FLOWER . . . .

The symbol of the lotus flower and meaning thereof depicts 'life everlasting'. Its seed first takes hold from beneath the deep watery pools of darkness. Deep within the muddy waters its bud seeks the light from above. It strives and struggles as it stretches beyond measure. Then finally it ascends to the surface above clear waters, out of darkness into the light. Its petals unfold and bath in the warmth of the suns radiant sunlight. Our life is likened to the petals of a flower unfolding; until our struggles are finally rewarded with the petals of life's full blossoms.

Several years after my near-death vision, I chose to be baptized in a local church with the emersion of water in a baptismal chamber. Many familiar faces surrounded us as we wore long white cotton robes. We each took our turn ascending the steps into the pool of water. Once the baptism was complete, there was a celebration of anointing prayers. I remember one elderly grandmother coming up to me. She told me that God was showing her in the image of her mind's eye that my life would unfold like the petals of a flower. Oddly enough I pictured a pink flower in my thinking. When I received the knundalini rising I actually saw a pale pink lotus flower blossom forth from my heart chakra. The aperture of our heart opens up like that of a flower when it receives love. When we contemplate our own soul's anatomy, we can compare it to the flower of the lotus. Our soul is part of the true NATURE of the Universe. If you have ever observed nature, everything begins as a seed. When we embody the Highest Light of Christ Consciousness that Jesus taught us, our soul blossoms forth from within, literally like a flower. Though it seems difficult to comprehend in our limited logical thinking, it is true. I have seen it with mine own eyes and it is documented in the ancient texts as fact. Each life center blossoms forth with the petals of a lotus flower.

When this happens we are bathed in the warmth of the cosmic universal consciousness of Christ energy called Kundalini fire. This cosmic fire is the anointing of the Holy Spirit. In ancient teachings and books I have read, it describes the crown life center having within its lotus over 1000 petals or more. When I first experienced these phenomena I was perplexed to its meaning. I quietly sought out answers in my own curiosity, not telling anyone what I had experienced, not even my husband. I happened on a metaphysical spiritual book store one day while shopping near the waterfront near my home. I was completely amazed when I happened upon a book on your soul's anatomy. Right there in front of my eyes was a pictorial book explaining what I had spontaneously experienced without any prior knowledge of its being. Since most people cannot see these life centers within our auric soul body with the naked eye, I was one of many who did not have any previous knowledge of their existence. We know that electricity and magnetic forces exist in our present day technology. We just can't see them with our visual perception.

When we experience the Father God's energy first hand, our mind's eye can see from within. This is sometimes referred to as the third eye in our forehead. It literally is the etheric eye of the soul mind. This sixth life center transcends human logic, surpassing it to join with the higher consciousness of the universal nature of God. Our 'inner' sight transcends matter and limited self-ego; it opens our awareness of God's divine eternal nature. This energy guides us to an expansion of our physical mind into the higher planes of God's conscious thought. It places us in a sacred place which is referred to as the all seeing eye of God. Our mind and soul are now one with God's Divine Love. We have access directly with the Father God from within. We gain a personal relationship with the Father of the Universe. Basically your inner cell phone is connected. The heart strings of your soul are connected to the thoughts of the most-high God of consciousness. You are in a plane of UNITY with God. We now can spend time in quite meditation and listen to his gentle promptings of inner guidance.

The sixth life center which embeds the pineal gland inside your brain is in now in relation to that of light. It transcends karma. The fruits of this life center bring forth forgiveness for self and others. The seventh life center which embeds the pituitary gland transcends and purifies karma.

I would like to project here, that MEDITATION is the act of LISTENING. As I have read in the scriptures:

> (NKJV) Psalms 46: Verse 10> "Be still, and know that I am God; I will be exalted among the nations, I will be exalted in the earth!"

Being 'still' is the act of being quite in communion with God. If you can, taking time out from our daily life and spend quality time in quiet contemplation. Even if it is for a few minutes in the morning, or later in the evening after the children are fast asleep. During this sacred time set aside, you can access the divine thoughts of God. Turn the T.V. and music off as well as all electronic devices. Spend time in quiet contemplation. Listen to your subconscious thoughts as you direct your attention to the God source of your soul.

PRAYER is the act of ASKING for assistance with our immediate needs. ASK and you will RECEIVE the scriptures tell us. God does answer our prayers, in His own time and in His own way. His timing is perfect and ALL KNOWING. As I have said before, the highest form of wisdom is gnosis or a direct knowledge of divine truth; this knowing is accessed by experiencing God's love and presence in your life first hand in a personal way.

Each life center is described to radiate a band of color of the rainbow emanating in your soul's light body. As I have described before, the crown chakra at the top of our head opens forth with a lotus of a thousand petals or more once spiritually activated. This center dispels fear when activated with light. We transcend and return to the source from where we came, the source of God's consciousness. We are set free from all darkness within. Our mind has traveled from matter to embrace spiritual awareness. We have an internal radiance clothed in white light. We are in unity with the Divine Love of the Father God.

EXPERIENCE is our very best TEACHER. We learn God's power by personal experience. It is electro-magnetic in nature, sometimes referred to the fire of the Holy Spirit.

Western science is imprisoned within the framework of its limited intellect. Its mind is closed to the possibility of a personal God. You cannot scientifically conceptualize the alchemy and power of God's Spirit. God is not limited by our five basic senses as the study of science is incased within these five parameters.

In ancient time, the symbol of the dragon referred to our ego, or the dragon of the ego within. It's puffed up with pride and self-importance; ignorant of the deeper mysteries of spiritual truth. Beyond our five senses is the sixth sense, that of spiritual knowledge.

When we experience the power of God's light first hand, we are embraced in a state of bliss, raptured in the ecstasy of God's love.

This word **RAPTURE** is very significant here. The modern world of Christianity has mistaken this word to be literal in the physical sense. But once again I wonder if it is meant to be fashioned symbolically in conjunction with your inner being? When I had my out of body near death vision, my soul was taken up into a spiritual place, incased within a dimension of white clouds. The light from these clouds emanated a light that was brighter than I had ever seen, yet it did not hurt my eyes. It also emitted God's unconditional love.

The SECOND coming of CHRIST is within you. Remember the words of Jesus? "The kingdom of God is within you"!

It resides within your soul being called the Merkaba. The anatomy of your soul has the potential to be filled with God's everlasting Light.

As my good friend Italene Gaddis says, ...

> **"The flower blooms at different times and so do people."**

She expressed that "Father God" had given her these words for one of her many poems.

Her book: "From My Heart To Yours", is a collection of some of these poems.

Her statement is quite simple but yet profound.

It has been written that no man knows the hour or the day of the second coming of Christ. I wonder if this is because we each individually experience the anointing of the Holy Spirit at different times.

Now, 44 years later since my near-death vision, I not only comprehend but understand God's words to me, ...

"I will answer you, but in mine my own time".
. . . . In HIS own time, not mine . . . .

It has taken a lifetime of experiences and struggles to bud forth the blossom of enlightenment within my own soul. Everyone arrives to the birth of spiritual insight at different times! The mature gestation of the soul is different for everyone in a personal and unique way. Just as the fetus grows for a gestation of 40 weeks within the womb, our soul also has a certain gestational time which grows to maturity. What that gestation of time is, I am not sure. I think that it may be different for everyone on an individual basis.

FATHER, YOUR WILL BE DONE, NOT MINE . . . .

The seed of God's truth was planted many years ago within my younger mind at the age of 15. This seed took root within the darkness of my inner being. It then sprouted within the darkness of my soul until it grew to form a bud of truth. The bud matured until it opened its petals to its full potential. Basking in the fullness of the light it so deeply searched for. Our soul is likened to that of a flower.

Within the void resides darkness, yet it does have substance within its form. Its essence is dark yet thick like that of a light puréed pea soup. I remember this from mine own experience at the age of 15. I was at-one-ment with the void of darkness if you recall. The awakening of the Holy Spirit from within, blossoms forth through our seven life centers. Just as the earth has dark soil beneath our feet, seeds planted within it sprout forth. The human fetus takes form within a darkened womb in utero. It's protected and safe while it strives to grow to full term. It's born from darkness into the light; down the birth canal into a lighted room. Our soul when experiencing the second birth, rises upward into radiant light, returning to the light from where it first came. God awakens each one of us in a direct personal way. No two lives are the same; each soul has its own uniqueness. Each snow flake has six points in its star, yet each has its own lattice work of unique design. His patience and loving kindness endures through eternity. The Star of David is another symbol of spiritual significance; with six points in its formation. Each one of us is unique in our own way. The esoteric meaning of the symbol of the Star of David is called the Merkabah. Its formation is part of the sacred geometry of our Aura.

When I was much younger, I not only ASKED God what the Holy Spirit was, I asked God for **spiritual wisdom.**

> (NKJV): Acts 2 Verse 17 > "Your sons and daughters will prophesy," . . . .

So be it! God is my witness! It's taken a life time to learn the revelations and deeper meanings of the Holy Spirit of Light and Love. And I am still learning. Creation has no boundaries.

IMAGES OF THE HUMAN AURA . . . .

I encourage you to further your spiritual awareness of the pictorial images of one's soul anatomy. I have only briefly touched on the existence of one's seven basic life centers. There are many others in the totality of one's auric field.

I recommend the book: "The Chakras", by C. W. Leadbeater.

Enjoy seeking these spiritual truths on your own. The internet is teaming with images that validated my own experience first-hand. I feel fortunate that I experienced them BEFORE I knew of their existence. Look up the word Chakra as you perform a search on the web's internet. Type in: **images of chakras,** and you will see a plethora of imagery that will provide you with a greater understanding and awareness of their existence. "Seek and you will find", are wise words from antiquity.

THE CADUCEUS > THE WAND OF HERMES

Being a nurse, I cannot leave out this ancient symbol of the diagram used in the medical field called the caduceus. This icon is used for modern day medicine, as it has been for many years past in the history of mankind. Since I cannot provide you with a diagram at this time, I am going to ask you to look this symbol up for yourself.

It has been adopted from the ancient symbol called the Wand of Hermes, which originated from Egypt. Since it pictures two snakes within its formation, I have never liked this image. I have an aversion to the sight of snakes. Most people I personally know, including myself, think of the symbolism of the snake as evil.

Secondly, I have always been drawn to the archeology of ancient Egypt, yet I could not comprehend why so many of their statues included a snake in their headdress. Now that I have personally experienced knundalini first hand, and studied its original meanings in ancient texts, I now have a greater understanding of this ancient archetypal icon and its meaning.

The caduceus symbol depicts the journey of life force rising upward from our sacral base chakra through the PILLAR of life centers from our spine, up to the crown chakra that exists within our soul's anatomy. The snakes are only shown to show the **MOVEMENT** of life energy (crisscrossing) upward, back and forth while it weaves its way from the sacral base life center chakra, up to the crown chakra's life center. In Egyptian lore, the snake is the symbol of wisdom with the knowledge of both light and dark, good and evil. At the top of the caduceus are two wings. They symbolize the THIRD EYE in the pineal & pituitary gland of the 6th and 7th life centers once they have been activated. This life center in the middle of the forehead has two very large petals within its lotus that resemble the appearance of wings. This is where the (All seeing eye of God) resides with the expanded awareness of the sixth sense; also known as the psychic intuitive third eye. The pineal and pituitary gland provides one, when activated, with the ability to actually see the aura of one's own soul anatomy.

The ancients referred to this force as the **serpent fire.**

In Christianity, one refers to this same force as the **fire of the Holy Spirit.** It cleans away all the dross and imperfections within ones soul.

The wings of the caduceus symbol reflect the awakening of our third eye, the universal Christ consciousness of the Holy Spirit. These wings also signify the MARRIAGE or BALANCE of the Yin/Yang energy, the electro-magnetic bio-rhythms of the human body. This is where the sacred chamber or 'mound of olives' houses the Holy Spirit's awakening.

The snakes in the headdresses of the Egyptian statues signify the awakening or arrival of the magnetic force within the Yin energy to blend with the electric Yang energy force. If you notice, the snake is resting in the middle of their forehead. I wish to **emphasize** that personally did **not** use this symbol in my terminology while explaining the rising of this process of knundalini because I still have an aversion to the sight of snakes. I personally feel that the use of snakes used in ancient Egypt to symbolize the knundalini energy flow is a **misrepresentation for modern time** as we know it. The snake is the symbol of evil for most of those who follow the Christian faith in the western world of our current century; it is **NOT** a symbol of great wisdom as it once was thought of and depicted as, in ancient Egypt, for today's modern symbolism.

I encourage you to research, on your own, many other books on the anatomy of the soul. I have only skimmed the surface with the intent to bring the western world into the realization that they do exist and what they mean for the metamorphosis of mankind's soul; likened to that of a caterpillar to a butterfly. **Remember, that the temple of God is within you!** What I have described to you in minor detail is the truth.

THE EYE OF THE STORM

Every year I return to the lake where I grew up for summer vacation. This drive entails a 400 mile long road trip from the large city to the pristine mountain lake of heaven on earth as I call it. On one occasion, I and my young children happened upon a lighting storm circling the horizon. We had just crossed the Columbia River heading upward to the summit of the large mountain that graced its cliffs above. We pulled off towards the lookout station so we could see the beauty of the massive river below. At the pinnacle of this fantastic view, we noticed that there were shafts of lightning fingering down to the earth in all directions surrounding us. Yet we seemed to be in the center of the storm without cloud, rain, or wind. While there, we could see dark clouds hovering in the distant horizon circling in all directions with our panoramic view. Within these dark clouds numerous jets of electrical shafts were striking towards the earth. We were amazed at this fantastic view from above of this massive electrical storm below us. We got back into the car and continued on our trip. The storm lasted for several hours. It was still light outside, so our vision of the storm continued as we drove down the other side of the summit into the farm lands below. This trip usually takes about six hours to arrive at our desired destination in the car. We were already two hours into our mileage when we were capsulized within the protected eye (or center), of this extraordinary storm. We had to be in the eye of the storm because it continued during our entire trip. As we approached the city closest to the lake it began to rain upon our car as we traveled for a short period, then it stopped as we continued for one more hour beyond the city limits to my beloved home at the lake. I realized that we were just on the outskirts of the black clouds above. As we pulled into the carport that rests next to the beach, I noticed my neighbor Jeff sitting in his fishing boat not far from the front of his dock. I got out of the car, said "Hi" and let him know that there was a terrible storm right behind me. He didn't believe me since the lake water was calm and rested. By now the sky was dark and you could not see any signs of a storm coming. Yet by the time we unpacked our car to take our belongings up to the cabin, the strong winds descended. The lake was overtaken with huge wakes, making it difficult for Jeff to pull up his anchors. I saw him struggling to do so as his boat rocked back and forth amongst the huge waves. I waited to see if he made it home safely, before climbing the long stairway up to our beloved cabin on the hill. Thankfully he did, so all was well as we were protected within the confines of my parent's home sweet home. I loved the sound of the rain pelting down on the aluminum roofing. We turned off the light in the living room so we could see the lake light up with the lighting storms flash. It was a site to be seen: powerful, yet beautiful to behold.

The nature of the universe is a force of great power. I realize now, that we can compare our time in meditation with the higher power of God, like being in the protected eye of the storm. The storm can be likened to the struggles in our own personal life. The eye of the storm is likened to the peaceful place of meditative contemplation. It is secluded, protected, and hidden. It's sacred, holy ground, without wind or rain: complete peace. When our soul is in this quiet sacred place, we can then comprehend the thoughts of God's love and direction.

GUIDED MEDITATION . . . .

There is no right or wrong way to pray or meditate. This is what works best for me:

Place your mind in a quite space. Sit in a comfortable chair that allows your spine to be straight and upright in position. I sometimes like to place soft music on. My choice is the meditative music of the American Indian's flute; it has an earthy sound that relaxes ones soul, with only soft music, no voices present.

Pray for Godly protection before starting. Call in your personal guardian angles or spiritual guides appointed to you at birth. Ask that they place a protective cocoon of white light around you. As your feet touch the floor, think in your mind's eye that we as a people are connected to the earth. Then in your mind's eye, think of how Father God's love radiates his loving kindness to His children. Place yourself between these two aspects of electromagnetic flows of energy. Very slowly take long deep breaths. As you inhale, feel the energy of the earth rise up your legs towards the back of your spine, then up to the crown of your head. As you exhale, picture the energy from the warmth of God's love cascading down from the crown of your head, in front of your spine; back to the point of origin by your feet. Continue this with each breath while listening to the soft music. No words, just soft melodic tones of the flute. Enjoy the presence of both the female and male energies blending together within your soul. Bask in the presence of God's unconditional loving light. Enjoy this space as long as you wish. Pay attention to the call of God's spiritual thoughts. As you begin to feel His presence, you will recognize His inner promptings of etheric guidance within your own soul.

HEART STRINGS . . . .

We are all connected in the web of life. However, we have a deeper connection with some more than others. These heart-strings are connected at soul level. This is why a mother is so attuned with her own children. I attended a workshop called heart-strings before I had children many years ago. The instructor explained that this inner connection between us was taught to her from a Chinese spiritualist. She explained that there is an etheric string of attachment at soul level between key players in all of our lives. These etheric strings appear somewhat the same as an umbilical cord between a mother and her unborn child. I was told that we have the power to control the width of these strings when needed. She said that sometimes this in necessary if one has a controlling parent. This might be appropriate if one is to embark on a new life in College, or stepping out for the first time on your own. I was told to picture in my mind, this cord of attachment, as thin as I possibly could. Like that of a guitar string if necessary. As we do this, we let go of the controlling factor as they may have too much power over us. She also explained that these strings will always be present with our parents until we cross over to our spiritual home at the end of our life. The other key players in our lives would possibly be with a sibling that we are closer to more so than another. It could be a favorite Aunt or Grandparent, and of course our beloved children. I was also told that there is an attachment with those with whom we have had intimacy with in a sexual way; to those we are married to. These strings can be very painful when a divorce occurs, or when a child or parent dies within our lives. This attachment can be torn or injured when a major change takes place such as these mentioned. When I was first separated from my husband of twelve years I experienced this painful wound of separation within mine own emotional heart center. The marriage counselor we were going to was a New Age spiritual thinker. She too spoke of "strings of attachments" between both parties. She was one of these gifted people who could visualize auras and the anatomy of one's soul. She explained to me, that she could see the torn and severed cord falling out of my heart center that was once connected to my x-husband. She instructed me to pick it up and reattach the torn end of it while looping it back into my heart chakra. At first I thought she was a bit eccentric to mention such a thing because I couldn't see it with my own vision, but I went ahead and tried it. I could feel it, but I couldn't see it visually. To my surprise the emotional ache in my heart went away. As the counseling session continued she explained to me that this cord which had been attached to my husband for so many years kept falling out of my heart center. She had me reattach it several times. Each time a painful memory appeared in my emotional body, the cord would reappear as if severed and torn. I soon took notice within my mind's eye and continued the etheric practice she taught me. It helped a great deal with the process of self-healing. I prayed that God would heal my heart from this terrible pain that I was feeling at soul level. As I have learned, TIME heals everything. In time, I have learned to detach myself from my X-husband's energy and become mine own person; much stronger that before. No longer co-dependent.

There are other times when those who are close to us can injure our heart's emotional well-being with unkind words or actions. When this occurs, it is wise to place distance between yourself and the other involved. There may be a time when God will ask us to forgive them, but the pain of their actions still remain within your heart's memory. It's as if their harsh words have attached to our heart's center like a painful barbed hook. A wise grandmotherly women once told me that when this occurs, to place your own hand over your heart. She then guided me to imagine that you are literally picking up the hook out of your heart; as you do so, in your mind's eye, imagine placing a white or pink flower at the end of the hook. Then visualize sending it back from where it came. Before doing this practice, you bless the flower with spiritual love and light from Christ; then say, "I forgive you", or "may God bless you with His love". As you send back this attachment, you inform it that it cannot reattach. "I release you". If need be, in your mind's eye, pick up an imaginary shied of protection and place it in front of your heart so it is literally impossible for it to reattach. Scriptures teach us about taking up the shield of faith and to put on the armor of God so that the fiery darts of the enemy will not overtake you.

I admonish you to look up the biblical scriptures in EPHESIANS: Chapter 6: Versus 11 through 17.

Be an active player in the health of your own soul. Meditate in quiet contemplation with God's help. This helps the blockages in our life centers become healed. We each store painful memories within our soul's anatomy. It's time to release them so they don't have power over you anymore. As the light of Christ's Love takes place within our souls, the pain and darkness is replaced with light and loving kindness. The warmth of God's radiant Love will fill the cup of your heart with healing waters as you meditate; all the cobwebs of past memories fade away into oblivion as you drink in God's Love. You may not totally forget them, but the pain is no longer attached. Place your hands together in front of your heart as if they were in a cupped position of prayer. Open them up as God's Love cascades from the top of your crown downward. Let the healing waters pool into your cupped hands. From there, envision the cleansing waters pour into your heart chamber; turning the darkness into LIGHT. Close your eyes as you do this and let the healing take place in every cell, nook and cranny of your heart. Drink in the healing taking place. Allow it to seep into every part of your soul within a cocoon of white light inside and out.

I admonish you to research many other books on the subject of the anatomy of the soul. I have only skimmed the surface to bring the Western mind to the realization that auras do exist and what they mean for the metamorphosis of mankind; likened to that from a caterpillar into a butterfly.

POSITIVE THINKING . . . .

. . . . When my marriage was quite young, we were blessed to go to a positive thinking seminar. We also purchased several teachings on the subject to include creative visualization. It was a wonderful experience, and it taught us to think outside of the box. We also learned to accept new ways of thinking in our everyday lives.

We learned to view our "self-talk" and to analyze how we spoke to ourselves in our inner thinking processes. It helped me in my everyday job process of nursing, so when we learned something new we would learn to react in a positive way. They taught us how to accept professional criticism in the work place without becoming defensive. I learned to respond in a positive response such as: "Thank you for the feedback, (NEXT TIME) I will incorporate that into my way of thinking. I also learned to communicate what I wanted, not what I did not want. Such as the time I taught my children to stay in the yard to play so they would be safe. If you tell them not to go play in the street, that is exactly what they will visualize in their mind is playing in the street. So, instead you tell them to play on the grass only, so that they will be safe.

We also learned creative visualization in our lives. Basically whatever you wish to accomplish in our life can be done first by visualizing yourself actually doing it in your thinking. Then to actually continue towards your goal until you actually make it happen. What you intend can become a reality if you focus on it until it comes to pass. I used this teaching to help get over my stage fright. They had asked me to teach the baby bath class at work in the local hospital that I worked at, but I was too scared to get up in front of the crowd of people. I knew all of the questions and answers, but actually standing up in front of a room of twenty or so people was quite intimidating to me. I used the ideas that they taught us, which were to think of the process in your mind of actually performing the goal at hand. I pictured myself standing up in front of the classroom with a teaching flip board to guide my teaching process. I had it all planned out. So I finally began to teach the class, at first with one other nurse as a twosome. Then eventually I began to teach the class by myself without any stage fright. The process was a great confidence builder. We can do anything we put our mind to.

Even though we learned so many wonderful positive thinking techniques, it still did not save my marriage . . . .

LESSONS OF LIFE IN YOUR OWN FAMILY; LIFE IS LIKE A GAME OF CHESS . . . .

. . . . You can make what you think are the right choices in your own life, but you can't make the same choices for someone else. You cannot control what other people choose to do. Life is like a game of chess. Everyone has free will to make their own choices. This is what this earth plane is all about > free will. However, what another person chooses to do can have a great impact on your own life. I had always thought that my life would reflect the same long-term marriage as my grandparents and my parents. They both were married from forty to sixty years during their life. Divorce was not an option; nor was it even thought of. In my mind I had made the right choices. I was lucky enough to have the right spiritual direction in my life as a very young teenager. So I was not a wild child who made poor choices in life. However, I had been married for twelve years when I was faced with becoming a single parent. My husband and I were the same age. We didn't get married until we were twenty eight years of age. We had our first child at the age of thirty-six and then seventeen months later we gave birth to our second child. When my son was only four years old and my daughter was two our marriage dissolved. It was the best thing that we could do for our children at the time. I do not regret it under the circumstances.

I did however place within the divorce papers that we both had to attend parenting classes. We chose to attend the same class so that we could be on the same page with our parenting skills. We did not remain close friends, but we worked out a civil parenting plan. I was lucky enough however to have a mother-in-law who had a career in social work and a sister-in-law who taught elementary school. I learned valuable lessons from both of them on how to raise children. My mother-in-law had told me that if she had it to do over again, that she would never tell her children the phrase: "bad boy, or bad girl". Instead she told me that she would have said "I love you, but I don't like that", or "I don't like what you are doing". I agreed with her, so our children did not grow up thinking that they were a bad person inside their soul if they made a mistake. It is important that they think of themselves as a (good) person. It's important that they know the right behavior that we except from them. As I explained before, we need to let them know what we expect, not what we don't want. In other words, if you say to your children, "Don't play in the street." They picture in their mind's eye playing in the street. So the best thing to say is, "Play only on the grass". They then picture in their minds eye playing on the grass. I would explain to them why, and tell them that I want you to play only on the grass because I love you and I want you to be safe. If you play in the street you could be squished like a bug by a car, and I don't want that to happen. And of course if they did play in the front yard, which was seldom, I was always with them. We spent most of our time outdoors in the fenced back yard. When they did learn to ride their bikes on the street in front of our house, they were older and knew their boundaries.

REFLECTIONS IN THE MIRROR . . . .

Reflecting back to my own childhood at the lake, I recall a day that seems to stand out. At the bottom of our tall stairway from upstairs leading downstairs is a tall oval mirror. It took the place of my crib when my parents built on the new upper addition to our home at the lake. I was about ten years old when one day I walked downstairs to find myself alone in the house. As I stepped down on the last step I found myself gazing into the mirror. I especially looked straight into the reflection of my own eyes at the person that I had become and thinking to myself: "I am a good person inside my heart". It's so important to know ourselves and to dwell on who we are as a person, who we choose to be as we live out our lives. I am glad that my parent's too did not use those phrases of "bad girl", or "bad boy" as we were growing up.

TIME OUT . . . .

My sister-in-law taught me to purchase a timer and to place something that they valued on top of the refrigerator if their behavior needed correction. Most little boys are NOT going to sit still in a time-out chair when they are very little, especially my son. That skill worked very well. She taught me to use the timer for one minute per age of the child. So if they were three years of age my son's favorite toy was on top of the refrigerator for three minutes. It worked like a charm for many years.

The parenting classes we took taught us to use the two magic words, IF and WHEN.

"WHEN", was used when we wanted to represent a reward for desired behavior.

"IF", was used when we needed to represent a consequence for unwanted behavior, that was not harming to the child.

This technique worked for my son many times. He never wanted to put on his seat belt in the car as he got older.

I use to say to him:

> "WHEN you put on your seat belt we will go; IF you
> don't we won't".

I used colorful stickers to reward good behavior while placing them on a weekly calendar. My children would then see the sticker calendar taped up on the wall in their bedroom or in the kitchen. When they got enough stickers they could have a secondary reward. My plan included rewards on a menu at the bottom of the calendar when enough stickers were earned for certain goals. Going to get ice-cream or going to a movie, purchasing a toy, etc. They got to choose the menu items that they wanted to achieve. It gave them incentive to learn and obtain a reward for good behavior. It even became a game to learn how to clean up the play room and earn more stickers. It not only built up their self-esteem, it provided them with the tools of feeling an accomplishment of becoming a winner in life. It taught them success!

When they were very young, I enjoyed spending time with them; getting down at their level on the floor, and actually playing with them every day. I would complement them and say to them: "You're good at that", building up their self-esteem. When you play with them, let them be the ones to control the playing not us. Build up their self-worth; do not tear down or criticize them in a way that is damaging to their worth as a person. Let them know that you love them and tell them so every time you feel it in your heart. It's a love that causes no harm to them or to you.

WHEN I SAY NO I MEAN NO . . . .

. . . . My son had a hard time taking no for an answer when he was very young. He would throw a terrible tantrum when he did not get his way. One of the phrases my sister-in-law gave me from her training as a teacher was to say: "I promise I won't change my mind". That technique worked sometimes but not always.

My son would drive me crazy when we went to the grocery store together. Since I was a single mom, I did not have the luxury of leaving them at home with another caring adult, so I had to take my children with me wherever I went. He would ask for everything under the sun in the grocery store; when I said no he would hammer me with his request over and over again. With the help of the parenting class I learned to say no, and then tell him I was going to turn my back and ignore him. No meant No! When I first tried it, we were at the checkout stand. He continued to ask for a particular item that he was heckling me about. I stooped down, looked at him straight in the eye at his eye level, and said: "No". I then told him I was going to turn my back. He continued to walk around to my front side and ask again. I said no again, while turning my back to him a second time. It took about five times before it finally worked! I had literally made a complete 360 degree turn until he finally gave up. I couldn't see him because I had my back to him. But I heard him say those magic words: "Okay mom". I pictured him shrugging his shoulders in defeat. To me it was a miracle! From that day forward I helped him break his begging pattern of manipulation. His teachers at school had commented to me that he would not take no for an answer either. I was not the only one who was being tested. Finally, this negative pattern of manipulation in getting his way was broken. Thank God for parenting classes I recommend them to everyone!

I learned that if you give them something in the grocery cart, not to take it away or change your mind before purchasing it at the counter. Once you give something to them, it was THEIRS! I personally feel that taking it away would only create an angry child and a rebellious spirit. It is best to promise something as a reward for good behavior while you're in the store, then to go back at the end of your shopping for the desired item when they have passed the test of good behavior. On one occasion my two very young children started to run all over the store in different directions without my permission. Once they returned, I left the entire cart where it stood and told them that I was leaving right now without my groceries. I let them know that they had better follow me because I was leaving to get into the car immediately. They knew I meant what I said, because they both followed me to the car. When we got settled into the car they started to question me about the gifts that they had received in the grocery cart. They pleaded that if we were to go back in that they would not run off like that again. My answer was: "No, not today . . . . But when we return tomorrow you can try again", "if you stay close to me and behave, you can get your promised items then". They were not very happy as I drove back home empty handed. I never had another problem like that again. We returned the next day to finish our shopping. They behaved like little angels.

Since I was a single parent I could only be a good mother. But I could not give my son the male company that a young boy needs on a daily basis. I became very active with cub scouts and the Boy Scouts of America. This helped my son form good healthy values, and how to become a good and contributing citizen within the community. I also was a girl-scout leader for my daughter when she was older. Both of my children grew up with the YMCA child care before and after school while I was working as a nurse within my profession. It takes a community to raise a child. The YMCA provided children's sports for the children when they were younger. The baseball games were in the summer evenings, so I attended every game. My children had a well-rounded life even though I was a working mother. They did however, pick up a few words and phrases from the other children at school that I did not teach them of course. I use to tease them and tell them that they must have been a truck driver in their past life, because I sure didn't teach them the discolored words that I heard come out of their mouths! Forgive me; I know that not all truck drivers have bad language. It was just a simple joke within my own family to teach them better ways of saying things in a wholesome way.

THEN CAME THE TEENAGE YEARS!

All I can say to that is that I am a survivor. We made it through. I was ready for another parenting class just for the teenage years, but it never happened. When we had sibling rivalry I would sit them down in the family room and have what I called a family time out. On occasion I would invite their dad to join the circle when he would come to pick them up for his parenting time with them. Even though we did not parent the children in the same house, we tried to stay on the same page in our parenting skills so that the children had some stability and could not play us against one another. It seemed to work for us. During what I called family time out, we would all sit in a comfortable chair in the family room sitting across from each other. I would let each child have their own turn to vent their point of view and recent frustrations. We would talk about how each person's actions affected one another in the family. I was never sure if it really made a big difference, but I think it did help bring any problems to the surface. At least my children felt they were heard. Later in their high school years the sibling rivalry finally subsided. Both my children get along very well now and actually love each other very much.

I DON'T PLAY FAVORITES . . . .

My daughter use to say to me in front of my son: "You love me the most don't you mom?" I would never, never agree with her and let her know that I did not play favorites! I did say to her however, that she was my favorite daughter and that her brother was my favorite son. I expressed to them that I loved them both to the very depth of my soul in different ways, and that a Mother's love encompasses all of her children no matter what. There is enough love to go around for everyone!

My daughter was an easy child to raise, however when the teenage years arrived, we would often but heads. I often had to walk on egg shells and be very careful what I said. The sensitivity and irritability was quite thick in the room on a few occasions. There were times I just had to walk away while putting "myself" in time-out in my own room. It seemed to help me calm my mind, and emotions. I did not have a supportive husband present in the home to help with the responsibility of raising the children. On a rare occasion when the children were in high school and much older, I might even drive to the nearest book store, get a coffee, and sit down with a good book for some quality time alone. When I arrived home I would sometimes find a written note on the bread board in the kitchen that said I love you or a note of apology. Sometimes the best thing is to just walk away and say nothing. There were other times that I heard the words: "I hate you". I had never said that to my own mother, so it was very hard for me to hear those words myself. As I said, I did not have a supportive husband or partner to help me raise the children so I was on my own. I wondered, "Where did I go wrong"?

My response to that one was: "I will always Love you no matter what, but I don't like what you are saying or doing right now. Or, "I love you, but knock it off because no mother should ever hear the words you are speaking to me right now." "I deserve to be treated nicer because I love you the most."

And of course those were the early teenage years that this occurred. Most every teenager goes through this emotional separation from childhood to adulthood. We all grow up eventually; it takes a lot of patience and endurance one day at a time. I must have done something right, because both of my children are wonderful contributing citizens and in their twenties now; we are very close and speak to each other often. It was all worth it. I love being a parent and would do it all over again if I had the chance. None of us are perfect parents. At least I haven't met one yet. It's important to apologize to our children if needed. It helps them realize that we truly love them and that no one is perfect. I promise, these younger challenging years of growing up will pass and our beloved children can become beautiful, contributing adults. I am very proud of both of my children and who they have become.

MY MOTHER WAS A GOOD ROLE MODEL . . . .

I have never forgotten the words that my mother said to my brother when he was leaving home for the first time to go to college.

She explained to him: "As long as there is a roof over my head; there will be a roof over your head if you need one."

This world can be a pretty scary place when you are first branching out on your own. It's nice to know that if we need to move back home until we get back up on our own two feet, that we are welcome to do so. On one occasion I did so myself for a short period of time. It's important to be there for our children of ALL ages when life takes its twists and turns. Our children need their parent's advice and kind words as life takes its course. In turn, I say to the youth of our world, to honor your father and mother and show them the respect that they have earned. Then, when you need them the most, they will be there for you with open arms. And if that parent that you need is not a helpful factor in your life, then ask God to place someone else into your life to take the place of a helping hand when needed. The Mother and Father of the universe are also present and waiting for you to ask them for their help and assistance on your life's journey.

TAKE ONE DAY AT A TIME . . . .

It was not an easy task being a single mom and working full time to make ends meet. But my children never went hungry and they always had new shoes and new clothes when the school year started every year. When they were young, I frequented the thrift centers and sometimes provided them with used clothing. Most of the females in my extended family were stay-at-home moms. I was the exception to the rule. When I first faced the fact that I would be parenting by myself it was overwhelming. Their father and I had been married for a total of twelve years before divorcing. Our children were only ages two and four when this separation took place, so I had many years ahead of me as a single mom. I realized that it was too stressful to think too far ahead. Many a night I would cry myself to sleep, but I just kept going. There were times that I just wanted to give up, but I wouldn't allow myself to get depressed. So instead, I took one day at a time, one week, and one month. I just kept going from day to day and took care of that ONE day's business at hand. Somehow all the bills got paid. They were not always on time, but they did get paid. There was always a roof over our heads with food on the table. If I had to pay a certain bill a little late in order to have food on the table I did so. I kept the house and made the mortgage payment until I sold it after my daughter graduated from High School. It was important to me to keep them in the same school all the years they were growing up. I was able to do that when I was growing up, and I felt that it was important to have them do the same if at all possible. It provided them stability and a sense of belonging. I love being a mother and enjoy my children very much.

Life was happy despite losing the game of chess for a perfect family life with their father. Everyone's choices in life will affect each other's. You cannot control the other person's choices, whether they choose the light or the darkness.

What is right for them may not be on the same page as yours. It's our own responsibility to make the best of the situation and to continue on. I believe in keeping a positive attitude about life no matter what kind of curve ball life throws at us.

SUICIDE IS NOT AN OPTION . . . .

From some of the near-death experiences that I have read about previously, there are those who had tried to take their own life. In retrospect, they were happy that they did not accomplish this most dreadful deed. They came back with a new understanding that it is not only wrong to take someone else's life, but that it is also just as bad to take your own life. All life is sacred including our own. Some of the books I have read have explained that sooner or later, if a person does take their own life, they are sometimes caught between worlds in what they call the bardo. Bardo means a transitional state, or an in-between state. Some refer to it as purgatory which is a level of like-minded souls. They soon realize that they will have to return again in another life time with similar circumstances until they pass the tests of life. On the other side of the veil, we cannot advance to a higher vibration of the various cities of light until our soul's evolution is able to contain it. Have you ever heard of the seventh heaven? Once there, you are the closest to the throne of God's pure Loving energy; so whatever happens in our life time, its best to endure it to the very end, asking for God's help all the way. I've made it this far, so I certainly do not want to start over again!

REGRETS . . . .

Looking back there are occurrences in my life that I wish I could change. I would have chosen differently. When I was in middle school, I was very shy around boys. In fact I was painfully shy at this time of my adolescent years. Somehow, I was taller than most of the children in my class so that did not make it any better. There was a family that included three young girls that would rent a summer cabin at the lake every summer. They lived close by my home on the lake, so we spent many days swimming and water skiing and baking ourselves in the summer sun; trying to get the perfect tan. If we ran out of baby oil, we would put butter on our skin to obtain a good tan. I had such fair skin that I often looked like a cooked lobster in the beginning of every summer. I looked forward to seeing this family every year. One year, they even rented a horse to ride on the back roads. That horse especially liked to wade in the water of the lake; we all had a great time in each other's company. As both of our families grew up they stopped coming out to the lake in the summers. Until one summer, my good friend returned her senior year of high school after graduating. With her she brought a close girl friend from school and two young boys from her graduating class. She explained to me that these boys had been drafted to join the Army in the Vietnam war. So this was their last really nice vacation before being sent off to the other side of the world. She came to the lake that summer without the rest of her family, so they did not have a speed boat to go water skiing. She had explained to me that they would like to take the boys skiing and requested if I could take them the next day. Of course I said yes; I was actually looking forward to it. She was older than me, so she was in a different place in her life than I was. She was obviously not shy around boys as I was at the time. The next day, It was getting late in the mid-day after twelve o'clock, so I wondered if they were still coming. Then finally I saw a small row boat approach my dock with the two boys who were very eager to go skiing. But she and her girlfriend were not in the boat with them. They had come alone. I felt so uncomfortable around these young men with whom I had only met the day before. My shyness around boys encompassed me; I told them that I could not take them skiing. I had hoped that the girls would have come with them so we could have a nice day together. The boys asked if they came back later with the girls would they be able to go skiing then. I was sooo shy and uncomfortable, that for some unknown reason the word: "No" came out of my mouth. I was afraid to take them skiing by myself. They left, rowing back to their cabin down the lake rather depressed. I had hoped so deeply that my girlfriend would have come with them. The boys expressed that the girls had warned them not to come see me without them. They explained that they just could not wait any longer. They were so excited and eager to go skiing. For some reason my heart just froze up with fear and shyness. This was before my near-death vision, so I did not have the perspective in life as I did later. I had hoped that she would still come over with her friends later that day to go skiing. I waited all day but they never came. I never saw or heard from her again. To this day my heart aches with the emotional pain of that day. I wish so very much that I had gotten in my motor boat and taken them all skiing, I was too shy to do so and was not emotionally mature enough to do so. I have always regretted not taking that second step, going to their cabin despite my shyness. I too have wondered through the years if those beautiful young boys came home from that terrible war alive. Today, when I think about it, tears run down my cheeks. I also think back as an adult how horrible that war really was. I think of my own son and how much I love him. I can only imagine the pain and suffering their families felt when their sons were shipped off to a war without the knowledge of their promised return. Sometimes it's what we don't do in life that matters. It's called the omission of sins in the Bible. I have prayed for forgiveness in my own heart, but I have never been able to completely forget what happened that day. I still feel the pain of my own actions of doing nothing and not following through. Cell phones and texting did not exist in those younger years. Their little cabin did not house a home phone either. Communication was not as easy as it is today.

Looking back, this is a reminder to reach out to those who need us in that given moment of need. You can't go back later to change the course of your actions if you lose that one chance. I am still learning to seize the moment without hesitation. Don't hold back in fear. Reach out with loving kindness when given the opportunity.

FULL CIRCLE . . . .

So now that my children are grown, have moved out on their own, I find that my life is now my own again.

Believe me, there is light at the end of the tunnel. I have been feeling the empty nest syndrome which is somewhat of a shock at first. But it has not taken too much time to refocus my directions and interests to claim back my own identity instead of that of a mom and a care giver.

All my life I have sought the truth in spiritual matters. Even in my fifty plus years I still don't have all of the answers. I think that I have figured everything out in my mind, and then something happens that perplexes me again. I have come to realize that the best thing to do is to have a simple faith and trust in God. Within my heart I know there is a higher source above our human understandings. The perfection of God dwells in the purity of etheric consciousness outside of physical manifestation. In the third dimension we live in duality of light and dark; good and evil. Our souls come to experience both to adhere to the choices we make on our journey of soul evolution. I know without any doubt, in every cell of body, mind, and soul, that there is a loving God-source directing our path; we simply need to ask for help and direction. Beyond physical manifestation in a spiritual energy form, I experienced that the God-source is the pure energy of Creation. When the bible says we are created in God's Image, I suspect that the image is of our soul base, not necessarily our physical form. It is the source of where my soul originated. We are all connected from this original source. We are a spark of energy that has come to experience physical life with limited knowledge of the human body.

We have chosen this human life to learn spiritual truths starting afresh with a clean slate. Within free will to have the chance to create whatever we choose to become. Whether its music, healthcare, engineering, business, etc. etc. Everyone has a passion or a gift. It takes time to find your life calling. We learn from each other.

The God-source of Creation is in the form of etheric energy of pure consciousness. Our souls are made of the spark or offshoot from this core energy. If we only knew or continually experienced perfection we could not truly appreciate it. So our souls choose to experience forgetfulness as we blend with the human body and mind. We come to this beautiful jewel called Earth to the third dimension called duality to learn the attributes of truth through adversity. Through trial and error we often learn from our mistakes.

Have you ever prayed to God for something and it never comes to fruition? Sometimes our prayers are answers later in life yet sometimes years have passed and still no answer has been given. I suspect that my answer was and still is "No". I have to trust that it has been for my best interest. Or maybe it was within my soul contract. I have grown very strong within my soul as a single female. In the course of time, it was tradition that the woman stayed home while the men worked and took care of the family. Yet now in this generation within America and around the world, women can be just as educated as the men. We can earn a living by ourselves without depending on someone else to take care of us. I must say it is very liberating. We are not co-dependent on another person. We can stand on our own two feet and survive as a single entity. At the same time, I believe our precious young children desperately need their mother at home in the preschool years of their upbringing. They need a loving parent to be present to greet them when they arrive home from school. My daughter use to beg me to be home after school, but I couldn't. Instead, they attended the YMCA before and after school. When they were too old to go, they then escorted themselves home from the bus after school. I wouldn't arrive until much later. By then, they had made their own dinner or microwaved something to eat. I fear that the family unit has disintegrated into something that is no longer as wholesome as it once was. The children are the ones who suffer. I am sad that the family unite has been turned over and become disjointed by taking the mother out of the home into the work place.

LETTING GO OF ANGER . . . .

Anger is born from the experience of betrayal or from being victimized against your own will. The branches of anger are the heart felt pains in the depth of your heart and soul. Those branches can grow into bitterness, hate, and self-pity. When I first realized that I was going to become a single mother after being married for twelve years prior, I was consumed with an overwhelming anger. The hurtful wounds of emotional trauma can bind you or shackle you with emotions of anger, to include an unforgiving heart. Generally speaking, a person can be overwhelmed by anger due to the injustice that you have just experienced in the course of your life's path. For me, it was facing a life of raising my children by myself, without a supportive partner. This was certainly a curve ball being thrown directly into the face of my life's course. It was the death of the so called perfect family life with the white picket fence and happily-ever-after fairytale marriage. I remember speaking to one of my fellow nurses at work who was now on her second marriage. She had raised five children with her first marriage. I will always be thankful for the words that she shared with me. "You HAVE TO FORGIVE them or the anger will consume you from inside out, and make you a bitter person. You FORGIVE them more importantly, for your OWN SAKE, or the anger will destroy you. Her words rang truth to me. I knew that I could not hold this anger within my heart forever. I felt imprisoned within its clenched fist of heart felt pain. It was almost just as painful as the betrayal itself. For the healthiness of my own heart and soul, I did forgive. That does not mean that I completely forgot the occurrence or injustice. I can observe their actions, but not accept them for what they were. In other words, we can choose to be indifferent and detached from the situation. But we CAN FORGIVE the person. The bible explains to love the sinner not the sin. I didn't love this person anymore in a romantic way, but in the sense of their soul as a child of God. I basically released them to God's care. Within every one of our souls is a portion of God's star seed from the same God/Source. It just takes each one of us time to learn certain lessons over the course of time, to perfect not only ourselves but to perfect our discourses with others. It's a learning process for both parties. We have an eternity to work on this task.

LET GO AND LET GOD . . . .

So I have personally learned that it was best to LET GO of my anger, and LET GOD take care of the rest. I basically said to myself, "I RELEASE YOU", and the pain that you've caused me. In some instances I had to say I release you several times when bad memories would arise. At the same time I knew that it was in my best interest to set healthy boundaries to preserve my own well-being. I also felt it was important to proceed with respectful communication.

My motto was to:

"Make peace with the crows", keeping in mind,
not to throw fuel to the fire.
Ignore bad behavior; just walk away if need be and
NOT to respond.

LET GO and LET GOD take care of the bigger picture in the course of eternity. I learned to lay down my burden at God's feet and ask Him to take care of the soul lessons that the other person may need to experience. We too have learned lessons in the same process, sometimes by experiencing the life of hard knocks metaphorically speaking. We are not perfect either! We have our own lessons and karma. We ourselves can forgive, knowing that in due time in the course of eternity, everyone will eventually graduate to a higher level of awareness and understanding on how to treat our fellow man. It might not be in this particular lifetime however. By forgiving the other person, we eventually put our faith and trust in God, that He will take care of that person's soul evolution in His own time. We all learn at our own pace.

FORGIVENESS . . . .

Forgiveness for me is a mind-set or a decision to forgive someone regardless of their offense to me or to someone else. To Love the sinner but reject the sin is when unconditional love steps in to transform the situation. We all make mistakes in the course of our life. We too need to face ourselves and ask the source of our soul for a second chance to make things right. The fact that we often learn our greatest lessons in life by the mistakes that we make is a humbling experience, yet the most profound. When this occurs in our own lives, something deep within our heart receives a feeling of thankfulness and peace. We become more humble, and less self-righteous. We can then turn around and forgive others more readily. Once we forgive, then our hearts are open to be filled with God's healing. Remember to let go and let God take care of the soul evolution of everyone who has crossed your path. They too are children of God and will eventually grow to maturity in the course of eternity.

HEALING . . . .

As we forgive, ask the Holy Spirit of unconditional love to fill your heart's center with the balm of healing to cleanse away the pain. Release your emotional wounds to God's loving care. Ask the mother of the universe to give you peace and comfort. Place your presence within her heart; bath in the osmosis of her divine love. Imagine the Father of the Universe holding you in His tender loving arms like a blanket enfolding you. Open your heart to receive the warmth of His loving kindness. Picture in your mind's eye the healing waters of the river of life force, flowing throughout your entire inner being. Dwell here as long as you wish. Let the warmth of His Love soothe your heart in peaceful contentment. Let the Light of the Holy Spirit embrace your entire being like a cocoon of Loving Light. Let it expel all darkness within; be a beacon of light that shines for all to see. Walk forth with the Mantel of God's Holy Spirit clothed in the robes of pure white illuminating light.

GOALS . . . .

. . . . My favorite movie of all time is: The Sound of Music. Within this movie there is a famous song called Climb Every Mountain. The words of this song have great meaning to me and have guided my life in many ways. They explain to climb every mountain, ford every stream; follow every rainbow, until you find your dream. In other words, don't give up. Keep climbing the mountain until you have discovered your dream or accomplished your goal. You can rest along the path to the top of the mountain, but you never give up until you reach the very top.

BLESSINGS . . . .

As I look back in my life a few people stand out in my memory of time. I especially remember an acquaintance I had of an elderly Asian woman who had immigrated to the United States. She appeared to be worn by the hot sun. Her tanned leathery face was wrinkled, while her smile was missing several teeth. A relative explained to me that she had spent most of her life working in the rice fields for a life of hard labor. Since she could not speak English, we used simple hand language to communicate; we seemed to do okay. There was an inner beauty within her that shined throughout her personality. The love within her eyes surpassed that of her outer appearance. I recognized the Holy Spirit within her soul, shining throughout her entire being. As I served her lunch, she touched my arm to communicate something to me as she took an orange out of the bowl on the table. She then closed her eyes in prayer as she cupped the orange of fruit in her hands. I could see her placing her love and blessings into the orange. As she opened her eyes, she then offered the orange to me as a gift, and said in broken English: "Thank you". I was completely moved at soul level as I received her gift of love and gratitude. By pure instinct, I automatically bowed my head with a heart of respect; I offered her my loving smile as I received her gift in my hands and heart. I humbly said: "thank you" in return. I looked deep into her eyes and saw the Holy Spirit of love within her eyes and soul. God's love does not have boundaries; His love encompasses all cultures and religions around the world. I lovingly said thank you as I accepted her sacred gift, not only in my hands but into my heart as well. She moved me to the depth of my soul. If anyone were to ask me which was one of the most cherished gifts I have ever received in my life, I will say to you it was this heart filled orange. She gave me a piece of her loving soul.

THINK WITH YOUR HEART . . . .

. . . . When your heart is open to the Holy Spirit of God's love, you learn to be guided by an inner intuition. You learn to listen with your heart and act on its loving kindness. The greatest wisdom in the world is a deeper knowledge that encompasses not only the thoughts of our mind but the intuition of our heart. Those inspired hunches that come to us spontaneously show us that we are all connected in some way. The greatest lesson in life is not only how to love others but to learn how to love God and how to love ourselves. I am still working on this and always will . . . . Love has no boundaries.

> (NKJV) Mathew 22:
>
> Verse 36> "Teacher, which is the great commandment in the law?"
>
> Verse 37> "Jesus said to him, "You shall love the Lord your God with all your heart, with all your soul, and with all your mind."
>
> Verse 38> "This is the first and great commandment."
>
> Verse 39> "And the second is like it: 'You shall love your neighbor as yourself'."

MICHELLE PETERSEN COPYWRIGHT 2013.

END NOTES:

"LIFE AFTER LIFE", by Dr. Raymond Moody

"PROOF OF HEAVEN", by Dr. Eben Alexander

"CLOSER TO THE LIGHT", by Melvin Moore M.D. and Paul Perry, Learning from the near death experiences of children.

"LIFE AFTER LIFE" by Jim B.Tucker M.D.study of children's memories of past lives.

"JOURNEY OF SOULS", by Michael Newton, PH.D

"DESTINY OF SOULS", by Michael Newton, PH.D

"THE CHAKRAS", by C. W. Leadbeater

"HANDS OF LIGHT", by Barbara Brennan

"CHAKRAS FOR BEGINNERS", by Naomi Ozaniec

"THEORIES OF CHAKRAS: Bridge To Higher Consciousness", by Dr. Hiroshi Motoyama

"MANY LIVES, MANY MASTERS", by Brain L. Weiss M.D.

"LIFE AFTER LIFE; THE THEORY OF REINCARNATION", by Eustace Miles

"REINCARNATION FOR THE CHRISTIAN", by Quincy Howe, Jr.

NEAR-DEATH EXPERIENCE NDE, of Mellen-Thomas Benedict @ neardeath.com web site

"FORBIDDEN FAITH", "The gnostic Legacy from the Gospels to the DaVinci Code", BY Richard Smoley.

near-death web site and Edgar Casey ARE foundation

"THE INCREDIBLE YEARS", by Carolyn Webster-Stratton PHD

"From My Heart To Yours", by Italeen Gaddis

PACIFIC INSTITUTE OF EXCELLENT LEARNING, founded by Lou Tice; presenting: positive thinking seminar

Web sites:
"Edgar Cayce on the Book of Revelation": web site:
http://www.near-death.com/experiences/cayse10.html
Reincarnation and the Early Christians: web site:
http://near-death.com/experiences/origen06.html
"Reincarnation", "The Fifth Council", web site:
http://kuriakon00.tripod.com/reincarnation/fifth_council.htm

"Gnostic Gospels": web site:
http://en.wikipedia.org/wiki/Gnostic_Gospels

Wikipedia Dictionary: web site:
en.wikipedia.org/wiki/Dictionary
Wikipedia: web site:
www.wikipedia.org
"The Gnostic Society Library", "Cathar Texts and Rituals", web site:
http://gnosis.org/library/Interrogatio_Johannis.html

"The Cathars: Cathar Beliefs: Heaven, Hell, Reincarnation and the
Afterlife", web site: http://www.cathar.info/120117_heavenhell.htm

"The gnostic Society Library", "The Nag Hammadi Library, web site:
http://www.gnosis.org/naghamm/nhl.html

"Nag Hammadi", Wikipedia, the free encyclopedia, web site:
En.wikipedia.org/wiki/Nag_Hammadi

"Reincarnation and the Bible", web site:
http://www.near-death.com/experiences/origen03.html

Scriptures throughout the book are from (NKJV) NEW KING
    JAMES VERSION of the Bible.

"Flowers bloom at different times, and so do people".
Quote by Italene Gaddis

This is the lake where I grew up as a child, I refer to it as my: "Heaven on Earth"

The Earth has a Soul and so do We.

"My people have forgotten me,
so I reach out to All the People of the Land".

Our prayers are to be One with God and to be in Harmony
with the Creation of Nature.

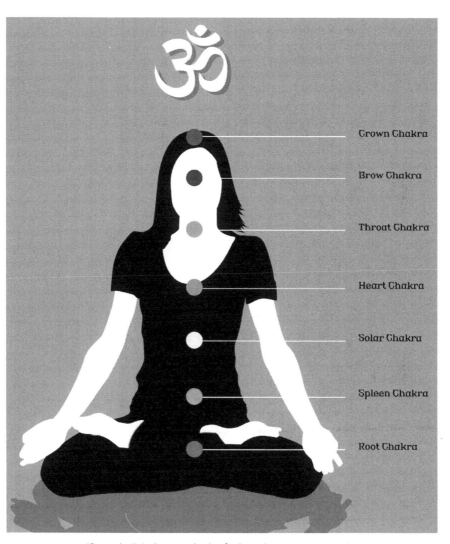

Crown Chakra

Brow Chakra

Throat Chakra

Heart Chakra

Solar Chakra

Spleen Chakra

Root Chakra

Female/Male symbol of the electromagnetic
bio-rhythms of the human soul.

Yin/Yang symbol

Reflections

Of

In Your Lifetime Follow The Light . . . .

Not the darkness

Contents

Words

Words do hurt more than sticks or stones;
They can cause years of sorrow and cause weary bones.
Don't speak the first words off the top of your hat;
You'll be sorry you said them,
because you can't take them back.
So be careful what you say;
It's best to walk away.
Hold your tongue for a while;
Then walk a few miles.
It's best not to speak out with strong words of emotion;
They only contribute to the chaos and commotion.
So when the storm has finally calmed down;
Please come around and find a common ground.
Don't contribute to the storms of pollution;
Rather meet half way and create a solution.
Words can cause feelings of love or of sorrow;
So choose love my friend and hold your tongue,
until tomorrow.

Walk away until the storm subsides;
When the clouds part, the right words will abide.
By then your words will be filled with love;
And if you permit, with God's inspiration from above.

MICHELLE PETERSEN 2012 > I dedicate this poem to Mordou
who also has a HEART of GOLD.

Forgive Me

I wish I hadn't said that;
Now I can't take my words back.
I spoke out of turn with strong feelings of emotion;
As soon as those words flew off my tongue;
I realized they took motion.
If only I'd waited to cool off my head;
I'd be much happier instead.
But no, I spoke off the top of my hat.
I didn't even think before my words went splat.
I come to you now with a heart of remorse.
Do you think you can forgive me all in due course?
Please know that I Love You deep down in my soul.
I never meant to harm you;
Those words should never have ever been told.
Please know that I will ALWAYS LOVE YOU
deep down in my soul.

MICHELLE PETERSEN 2012

Forgive You

I HAVE WIDE SHOULDERS,
A DUCKS'S BACK,
AND A WARM HEART.
Who am I, not to forgive you?
For I too have done my part.
As time goes by in the course of life;
We all look back and see that we too have caused strife.
We have said things and done things that we can't change.
We don't have the right to continue the blame.
Nobody is perfect and neither am I.
We'll have to pay later with karma says I.
What we throw out will come back in due time.
The fruits of our labor will reflect and shine.
Until one day, we hit our limit of remorse and say . . . .
I fall on my knees with a humbled heart, and pray.
I can't hold a grudge when I too have strayed,
Off of the path of righteousness that God has made.
I forgive you as God has forgiven me.
God has liberated us with the Holy Spirit, you see.

MICHELLE PETERSEN 2012

Reflections In The Mirror

Look into the mirror; what do you see?
I see mine own eyes staring back at me.
Who am I?
So I look a little deeper.
Within the depth of my soul I see a spiritual seeker.
I stare beyond the face staring back at me;
I feel within my heart a sphere of golden light.
It wells up with love within my second sight.
And I think to myself that: "I Am A Good Person".
Yes, there is a feeling of goodness deep within my soul.
And now I know who I really am . . . .
I Am A Good Person With A Heart Of Gold.

MICHELLE PETERSEN 2012

Teenagers

As a young teenager I was not a leader;
But I didn't follow the crowd either.
If I saw some people doing things I didn't believe;
I quietly walked away from the crowd,
and did not partake of their deeds.
YOU DON'T HAVE TO BE A LEADER,
BUT YOU DON'T HAVE TO BE A FOLLOWER EITHER:
They may call you names the very next day;
and refer to you as:
"Goody two shoes", but that's okay . . . .
Because I don't have anything to prove,
Other than to preserve my own person.
To make better choices that preserves,
who I am inside my own soul, and who I choose to be.
So there are times in my life that I watch and observe;
But I don't choose to partake of that which I see.
I HAVE NEVER BEEN A BORN LEADER,
BUT I CHOOSE NOT TO BE A WEAK-MINDED FOLLOWER EITHER!

MICHELLE PETERSEN 2012

Protect Your Own Soul

Protect your heart-soul with all your might;

Turn away from darkness and turn to the light.

Ask God for the answers that your soul is searching for;

Life's destiny will follow with God's guidance as before.

Speak kind words to yourself and to others;

Kindness goes a lot farther than harsh words my brothers.

Hearts will open up with a life filled with love;

Choose well your words and God's guidance from above.

MICHELLE PETERSEN 2012

The Dark Night Of The Soul

Endure the dark night of the soul; I promise it won't last.
Ignore it and you will see, a glimmer of new light
That will enlighten yesterday's past.

Wait another day or two;
Your burdens will lift and the clouds will part.
You will be filled with hope again;
And solutions will present themselves within your new heart.

Don't be afraid to ask God for help and guidance.
For when we ask . . . .
Then God's Angels can come to our aid with kindness.

Give your thoughts and feelings to a higher power of might;
And you will be filled with God's beautiful Love and Light.

MICHELLE PETERSEN 2012

Setting Boundaries

Setting boundaries is the key;
Not only for you, but also for me.
For I am worthy, to be parted from abuse;
The fruits of darkness I have no use.
I seek the light in all that life brings;
For the fruit of the light causes my heart to sing.
Surround yourself with a circle of friends,
Who think positive thoughts,
and fill your life with goodness that never ends.
What a wonderful life this can be if you just don't give up.
Then in time you will see that life is worth living;
And most people are very-very loving and giving.
Set boundaries with those who are negative and harming;
The fruits of their labor may be quite alarming.
It's time for you to stand up;
Simply walk away from that which is not deserving.
Stand up for what you believe in: Love and Truth,
Which is worthy of your deserving.
Setting boundaries, never to return;
Forging a new life, old bridges I burn.

MICHELLE PETERSEN 2012

Making Peace With The Crows

Don't you know that I won't add fuel to the fire?
I refuse to keep fighting, and would rather inspire.

Make peace with the crows;
Life is too short to be at throws.

I'd prefer a peace treaty, so in my mind I envision.
A communication, that does not cause division.

Let's find a common ground that we both can work with;
So when the storm settles, we can once more find bliss.

MICHELLE PETERSEN > written: 1994

Second Chances

Okay, you've failed this time around.
So what!
Pick yourself up and get off of the ground.
Don't be so hard on yourself!

Sometimes it's the teachers of failure that teach us the most.
We learn what NOT to do the next time around.
We can then make better choices that succeed and abound.

So try again and again until you find what works.
Success is just around the corner;
I promise it lurks.

God will redeem you from your fall;
Brush yourself off, and stand up tall.
The journey of life is filled with many second chances.
So put on a BRAVE HEART;
And have the courage to begin a NEW START.

MICHELLE PETERSEN 2012

Suicide Is Not An Option

Suicide is not the answer,
to run away from this difficult place.
Because you'll have to come back to start over
With a new name, and eventually a new face.
Even if life, serves you a curve ball of messes,
I've made it this far,
So don't give up now.
Or you will have to come back next Century,
To try again somehow.
Faith in God will help you through to tomorrow.
Don't you know, that God picks up
The broken winged sparrows?
For He knows what you need,
And will mend God speed.
He'll place you in the palm of his hands,
To Lovingly minister the Balm of Giliad.

MICHELLE PETERSEN 2012

Don't Give Up Today

Don't give up today,
For tomorrow is a new day.
So when you're crying in the middle of the night;
Just remember that the morning sunrise will bring new light.
It's a good thing to release your tears;
For the next day, you will see . . . .
that you have already released those fears.
The root of the matter can be seen with new light;
And you will be ready to put up a good fight.
So what do you have to lose?
Tomorrow everything may just work out.
And you may just discover what life is really about.
Give time a chance to prove that life is worth living.
And that your life is a part of that giving.
Stick around to see what's around the bend;
The road of life may just be your friend.
We all experience ups and downs.
Remember, this is not the end; our life can rebound.
Try again and again until you succeed.
Stand tall and become the man or woman that you wish to be . . . .

M. Petersen

.... Time is our friend, so don't give up;
New possibilities are on the war-front.
Time can heal all the wounds of life;
The storms will settle and calm the strife.
So give time a chance to prove;
That life is worth living.
And that your life is a part of that wonderful giving.

MICHELLE PETERSEN 2012

Wish It, Dream It, Do It

Follow the desires of your heart;
And wish them into being.
As long as they cause no harm to yourself or another;
In time it's worth the seeing.

What is it you wish to create in your life?
Certainly, a better world with no strife.
Focus your thoughts and dream them into being;
Then all of a sudden they will come forth into seeing.

It may take a while one step at a time;
While building one brick upon brick.
They will take form in due time.
Then right before your eyes,
your goals will transpire;
And all of a sudden, your life will inspire.

MICHELLE PETERSEN

Be A Good Friend

It's good to have a few friends in life;
Maybe one or two who will stick with you,
in the course of life.
They are there to help you in times of Joy,
and in times of sorrow;
And some times in the need of barrow.
We are all connected in the web of life;
So please don't add to the confusion and strife.
Reach out your hand to those who matter;
Your omission of sins may haunt you much ladder.
Your warm heart and kind words may be what they need;
They should not have to tell you, or to plead.
Offer your hand and help them to stand.
We are all connected in the web of life;
Create a world where there is no strife.
Hold hands with your brothers and no one will fall.
Together we stand;
We stand rather tall.

MICHELLE PETERSEN 2012

Curve Ball

So when life throws you a curve ball,
that you did not expect;
You scratch your head and think: "what the heck"?
You're shocked beyond measure and think
"Now what will I do"?
It's almost as bad as losing my shoes.
Then all of sudden you begin to think;
It's better to throw everything into the sink.
The unexpected twists and turns in the roads of life;
Can certainly cause us a lot of strife.
So time goes by, and you sleep on it at first;
And sooner or later a new solution will take birth.
So don't give up just yet;
You'll think of something I know, I'll bet.
You're faced with a new start in life;
A time to create, a time to put away all of the strife.
New beginnings are facing you now.
Stand tall and be strong; you can do it even though,
You may not know how?
Time will tell . . . .

M. Petersen

New thoughts will download;
Into your pathway along the road.
Keep going one step upon step at a time;
And God will lead you all in due time.
Success is just around the corner;
So stick around to see what's in order.
Life is worth living I know you will see.
Even when life throws you a curve ball;
And this just can't be!
Yes life can throw you off course at times;
BUT MAYBE A NEW COURSE IS JUST WHAT YOU NEED!

MICHELLE PETERSEN 2012

What Is My Passion?

What is my passion in life?
THE KEY IS IN YOUR HEART'S DESIRE.
You came into this life with a soul purpose.
THE KEY IS IN YOUR HEART'S DESIRE.
Think with your heart; . . . . And in due time you will know.
For in your life's journey, you will be shown.
What provides you with the spark of knowledge?
Is it music, or science, or going to college?
What do you wish for? . . . .
In the deepest trenches of your soul?
Your heart will guide you; . . . . And then you will know.
It might be the Art's, or writing a book;
Eventually you will find your nook.
Maybe your goal is to become a loving mother,
Or to become, ... a famous cook.
Whatever it is, there is no right or wrong;
As long as it makes you happy and fill's your life with song.
Let it be something that serves you well;
And serves mankind for all to tell.
Let it be something that you can be proud of;
For your passion in life is what you are made of.

MICHELLE PETERSEN 2012 > I dedicate this poem to Joseph Campbell.

Put Your Trust In God....

.... Are the words of wisdom spoken.
Acknowledging a higher power;
To receive help from a higher token.
There are times in our lives
that we can't carry the burden alone;
It's a good thing to cry out for God's help,
For He can lift our burdens to be shown.
When doors are closed in the pathways of life,
A window will open and bring new light.
Time can heal the pains of sorrow;
The tumultuous storms will cease tomorrow.
The Sun will rise and bring new life;
Let go of past failures and they will subside.
Look to the future; Try, Try again, until success takes over.
Not all is lost, there's a new day moreover.
Greet each morning with a prayer in your heart;
To take the right steps of God's guidance, we must.
Put your faith in God; for in due time, our steps will be guided.
For within Him, we place our trust.

MICHELLE PETERSEN 2012.

Soul Searchings

So why am I here on this blue jewel called Earth?
Though I am thankful my Lord, for choosing this birth;

Life is much harder than I ever had thought.
I think I've chewed off a bigger bite than I had bought.

I've come to stand strong, to form a back bone;
To prove to myself, that I can do it when shown.

I know I will make it, to the very end;
And walk away from life's course at every bend.

Knowing I gave it my very best;
I've proved to myself, that I can pass the test!

MICHELLE PETERSEN 2012

The Temple Of God Is Within My Own Soul

I don't need a church to seek God's direction;
God speaks to my mind and heart,
With His wisdom and perfection.
This doesn't mean we can't gather together;
And be a support to one another.
For after all, we are all brothers.
Just know that deep within your heart;
God will speak his truth to you from the start.
But first you must ask Him for the answers you seek;
Then He can bless you with what your heart needs.
His answers may come from His still-soft voice from within;
Or from the inspirations from a Holy Book
that you have read to begin.
Occurrence and coincidence just might take power;
And gently be placed in your pathway,
like the soft rain of a shower.
Your mind will be liberated; your soul set free.
To know we are really not alone;
In this journey of life, with God and with me.

MICHELLE PETERSEN 2012

Follow The Light
Not The Darkness

Make a choice in your lifetime to follow the Light;
Put on God's mantel dressed in white.

Be a beacon of everlasting Light;
The love of the most-high God will give you insight.

The pillar of light energy that stands in your soul;
Runs north to south, from head to toe.

Stand tall like a pillar dressed in white;
Join the ranks of the sons of the most-high God.
The Sons of Light!

MICHELLE PETERSEN 2012

Second Birth

How I love to feel the presence of the Lord within my soul;
My sins that gave me so much woe have vanished in the snow.
Please shed them off to Him my friend;
He'll give to you I know . . . .
Love and peace, I know you've never known;
And all your life He'll keep and guide your soul.
So release your fears and cares to Him;
He'll give to you I know . . . .
A life that is worth living, A joy you've never known.
Yes the presence of God's spirit brings me peace,
And this I know . . . .
That only you Christ's Spirit breathes life into my soul.
Give to Him your heart my friend;
He'll give to you I know . . . .
Love and peace I know you've never known.
And all your life;
He'll keep and guide your soul.

MICHELLE PETERSEN > written: 1969

Blossoms Of Life

Your life will unfold like a beautiful flower;
Until you see God's miraculous power.
God first created you as a small star seed;
Your life is sacred from the very beginning you see.
He planted your soul on an orb called Earth;
Then nurtured you until you gave birth.
You chose to come to live and to learn;
To be held in God's arms from a sprout to a stern.
Your soul searched and searched for life's meanings;
You've strived.
And your seedling burst forth like a blossom of Life.
Your life will grow from a seed to a bud;
Then all of a sudden, blossoms forth in full sum.

MICHELLE PETERSEN 2012

The Mantel Of Baptism

The true baptism is of the soul;
It's the Holy Spirit of God that fills you from head to toe.

Take on the mantel dressed in white;
Walk forth in God's righteousness and Light.

The sins of your soul will be washed away;
And God's direction and guidance is yours to stay.

The baptism of water is of the flesh;
But the deeper baptism from within,
Will help you pass the test.

The tests of life will still come your way;
But you'll have God's help to hold your hand along the way.

Invite him my friend into your heart;
And you will be given a brand new start.

Take on the mantel of the Spirit of God;
Then He will enlighten you for the answers you've sought.

Let the touch of God's breathe anoint the top of your head;
God's love will flow down from the crown of your head.

The anointing will continue right down to your feet;
Every cell of your soul will illuminate and greet.

Your heart will open up, and your cup runneth over;
Your body, mind and soul will be enlightened all over.

For when God speaks directly to your soul;
It's an experience that will be branded for eternity.
I know!

MICHELLE PETERSEN 2012

Hold You

Let me hold you with in my arms;
So I can embrace you closest to my heart.
Then the love from my cup overflows;
Will flow into yours and the emptiness you feel will hopefully part.
This life can sometimes drain our heart of all its stores;
We need to support one another,
So the next day we are ready to live life's journey once more.
When a child or a brother reaches out their hand;
It's important to stop our busy life, take measure and mend.
Then offer a lending hand.
All it takes is one small moment;
So stop what you're doing and cease the moment.
Offer a hug or wise words of Love;
Think with your heart, with God's will from above.

MICHELLE PETERSEN 2012

Apology

Why are you still holding a grudge?
It happened years ago; get over the smudge.
Well, that attitude that says:
"Just let go"!
May just need an apology, to lessen the blow.
The pains of what we've said years ago;
May still feel the arrows, that pierced long ago.
All it takes is a simple apology;
And the wound you caused can begin to heal.
Then the peace of mind and open heart,
Will bridge that friendship better still.
The balm of kind words will soothe the heart;
And never again will you be apart.
Better still, don't hang on to sorrows from days gone by;
Forgive the sinner, then Christ will surely be by your loving side.

MICHELLE PETERSEN 2012

Life Is Sacred

The moment that you realize that life is quite sacred;
Is the day you hold your newborn child
for the very first time.

This beautiful new life is cradled within your arms;
And your heart wells up with overwhelming love and new sight.

How can it be that this child sprang forth from me?
It's a miracle to behold; such a lovely responsibility.

To hold my sweet baby within my heart is like gold;
To cherish and guide this new life to behold.

MICHELLE PETERSEN 2012

What Is A Mother?

A mother loves her newborn infant,
With a loving and open heart;
She cry's the first day she returns to work,
Having to let go to impart.

So when her child is very young and clumsy,
And sometimes begins to fall;
A mother's love is always there to help them stand tall.

As time goes by, a mother loves her toddler every day;
She plays and giggles with them along the way.

She holds their hand and guides them,
To the very first day of school;
Though within her heart she worries that they will be okay,
In the path of life, consisting of many pools.

A mother loves her teenager even when they might say:
"I Hate You"!
Her response: "No matter what you say or do . . . .

"Be assured that I will:
ALWAYS, ALWAYS, AWAYS, LOVE YOU!!!"

M. Petersen

When you grow up and move out to make your own way;
Remember I am here to help you along life's way.

As long as I have a roof over my head . . . . So will you!
When the world is cruel, and you need my help instead.

A mother's love will never cease,
Even when the roads of life twist and turn around the bend;
Believe me she will always be there,
With her outstretched hands to lend.

MICHELLE PETERSEN 2012 > Dedicated to John and Julia and
to all the mothers and children of the world.

Hello My Friend!

What kind of Father would you like to be?
A Father that is present in his children's lives you see.
A man who is THERE . . . .
When his child needs him the most.
When the questions of life need answers, you can boast.
"Yes, I have been there and done that, I know how you feel"!
I can help you see what is really real.
The root of the matter is to be their friend.
To LOVE and laugh;
To heal disappointments that needed mend.
To LOVE and ENCOURAGE them;
To BUILD UP a child's interests you see.
Letting them know that they can grow up to be,
The very best person that they can possibly be!
Then tell them and say:
"I knew you could do it"!
"You have the courage to stand up and do it".
"And as you reach out to give them a high five;
You let them know you're a proud father,
when they succeed and strive.

MICHELLE PETERSEN 2012 > dedicated to All Fathers

Transmigration Of Souls

What is the transmigration of souls?
It's the steps of Jacob's ladder, the metamorphosis of old.

It's an old soul experiencing life once again.
An incarnation of new birth;
A new life to begin.

It's a second chance to set things straight;
To make wrong into right, of past failings and hate.

It's a step up the ladder towards a better way of life;
To return and make things right, with a new insight.

It's a chance to start over with a clean slate you see;
It's our soul's evolution to become all that we can be.
One life is not enough to learn all that we need;
It takes many lives to become star seeds.

MICHELLE PETERSEN 2012

Unfinished Business

My consciousness tells me,
I have unfinished business to take care of,
For tomorrow it could be too late.
Especially if my maker calls me home,
Before I empty my plate.

The skeletons in the closet,
That have caused me so much sorrow,
Need to be emptied out, before another tomorrow.

We don't always know what's the best actions to take?
But with God's help and guidance,
Amends we can surely make.

It might be a silent prayer within our own heart,
Or a letter of apology to impart.
Whatever it is,
Don't put it off any more,
Because God may call us home to His heavenly shores.

MICHELLE PETERSEN 2012

Crossing Over

Be careful what you believe;
Because your soul mind will create,
even if you focus on the statutes of hate.
When you cross over to the other side;
And this life is over, you cannot hide.
Better yet, think of meadows dressed in green;
And a mountain side of beauty, filled with pristine.
Follow the path to the top of the hill;
And ask God to meet you regardless still.
Review what you've learned, the good and the bad.
Sometimes our greatest teachers are the failures we've had.
Thank God for the chance to live and to learn;
Then take God's hand, even if you haven't earned.
Greet God with a humble heart;
Knowing that His outstretch hand will give you a new start.

Your life is the sum of good and some bad;
Celebrate the good and the happy times you've had.
Don't beat yourself up inside your mind;
You have an eternity to perfect TIME.
So follow the light,
when you cross over from this world to the next;
And your soul will be filled with God's loving best!

For the light that I speak of is blessed with God's love.
No matter what you HAVE . . . .
. . . . Or HAVE NOT DONE!

MICHELLE PETERSEN 2012

It's Not Your Time To Go

If it's not your time to cross over they say;
Miracles can happen to keep your stay.

Have you ever experienced an everyday Miracle?
That left you pondering of what happened was not physical?

I do believe our lives have a greater purpose;
In spite of our triumphs, or our failures.
Not only for me, but also for you;
God has a higher purpose!

And only when, our time and accomplishments have been settled.
Will our Holy Lord, call us home to the kettle.

If it's not your time to cross over they say;
Miracles can happen to keep your stay.

MICHELLE PETERSEN 2012

Mother Earth: Gaia Speaks

"MY PEOPLE HAVE FORGOTTEN ME,"
"SO I REACH OUT TO ALL THE PEOPLES OF THE LAND."
My veins of oil are like the life lines of blood,
That run their course throughout.
My oceans are the tears of joy & sorrows
I have shed for mankind, in the times of sand.
They in turn are teaming with life;
So don't pollute my clean waters, for they provide you
With abundant life.
Remember me my children; and know that I am real.
I have a soul as you do . . . . so live in harmony upon my land.
And don't use up all my resources, as if you were to steal;
For I too seek to be healed.
As I spin on my axis from day to day, from sunrise to sunset;
And from season to season.
Walk with me, as you live your life.
The Journey and destiny as your soul gives reason . . . .
A reason to live; to live and to learn.
Waste not your time on this precious Earth;
For life is too short.
MY LAND IS SACRED; as your LIFE IS SACRED.

M. Petersen

Learn to love one another, despite the differences of sort.
I wish you peace as you walk life's journey upon my land.
My people have forgotten me,
so I reach out to all the peoples of the land.
I offer you a peace-pipe of love and harmony,
As I reach out my hand.

MICHELLE PETERSEN 2012

Count Your Blessings

Count your blessings;
Say: "No", to depression.
Do not give in to self-pity;
It's a waste of your time and suppression.
Rather count your blessings;
And move on with life;
Find something else to fill up your time.
Start a new hobby;
Or exercise your body.
Discover your passion for life.
It's time to shed off the strife of past sorrows;
Look forward to life and a new tomorrow.
Discover your passion for life!

MICHELLE PETERSEN 2012

God's Eyes

I look up to God's face;
And I see the perfection of His love.

Though I am not worthy to look eye to eye;
I dare to do so, to learn what I lack.
So I can someday become more like His example from above.

Let the perfection of His love show me the way,
as I stumble along;
For through the example I see in Him,
my soul will sing a new song.

I seek to walk my life in such a way;
To not offend or to harm another.
To speak kind words of understanding,
To my sisters and my brothers.

MICHELLE PETERSEN 2012

Judge Not One Another

My grandmother use to say:
"Don't judge a person
until you have walked in their moccasin's".
This is a wise saying from yester-year,
Yet rings of truth for all to hear.
From some of the books I have read,
They say there is a pre-existence;
And that before our soul comes into this life,
We have a soul contract to learn certain lessons.
Our human brain may not remember;
But within the depth of our soul memory we carry
The hidden truths of our soul's evolution.
So be careful my friend,
for judgment may only add to the self-righteous
thoughts of pollution.
Some of our sisters and brothers may seem to have
A much easier time;
While others seem to struggle in the course of their life.

M. Petersen

It's all written down in the contract of time;
We all have a plan to live and to learn.
So be mindful of that plan,
before you speak unkind words of stern.
We all have a plan to live and to learn.
So we really cannot judge one another's course in life.
Because some may have chosen a life of hard knocks.
While others are resting this time around, with very little strife.
So even though my life is not perfect
there is no need for self-pity.
Because I have an eternity of time,
To experience all that my present life may be lacking.
Whether I chose, to live in the country, or to live in the city.
Keep mindful of the BIGGER PICTURE;
this life is only one of many . . . .

MICHELLE PETERSEN 2012

Inquisition

The inquisition set out to prove their position,
By burning books and innocent people I am told.
What a horrible, horrible position to uphold.
All in the name of the universal church of Rome.
The Romans past had put our Beloved Jesus on a cross for all to
see;
The politicians and religious leaders of that time,
wanted their laws, and belief systems, to take precedence to be.
They also targeted the Gnostics,
the founding Fathers of Christianity
Then the Jewish Hermetics and the order of Cathar's,
A Secret society.
The thread of commonality,
within these religious groups of three,
Was the belief in the Kabbalah and Jacobs Ladder you see.
Why would God give his children only one life to live?
And then from there decide if you go to Heaven or to Hell,
If one has not yet learned their lessons on how to forgive?
Some souls take longer to learn . . . .
. . . . During the time of eternity.

M. Petersen

It's not God who created hell
it was the ignorance of mankind;
And the sons of darkness who committed crimes.
The disciples fled to save their lives,
Deeper truths were hidden form the Roman public eye.
Yet truth has made its way through time,
In spite of all the political strife.
For now, we have come back to set the record straight;
And rid the world of all that strife and hate.
Jesus taught us to Love one another;
To be filled with the Holy Spirit, and to Love our Brothers.
Second sight and second birth;
To be filled with the Holy Spirit on this earth.
He came with forgiveness to set our inner souls free;
Yet the Roman soldiers hung him on a tree.
The cross did not put all to death;
Because his teachings have survived the test.
He rose again to tell us all,
To Love one another, to Love all.

MICHELLE PETERSEN 2012

Home Sick

I've been homesick for a very long time;
Ever since my experience, into the cosmic light.
I know I was placed here to do my part;
To contribute my life, with all my heart.
I've never forgotten the clouds of white light;
And I still yearn for God's Love and second sight.
I'm thankful for all my lessons I've learned;
Even when the road was bumpy with twists and turns.
I've LOVED every one of you with all my heart;
But now it's time for me to part.
Don't cry for me when I am gone;
Because I am now home, where I belong.
No more bills do I have to pay;
My work is done here and now I can say.
Job well done, I've done my best;
And knowing all of you I've surely been blessed.
I've cried, Loved and laughed with you along the way;
But now it's time for me to see a new day.
So now I go through the dimensions of space;
To a heavenly home; beyond this place.
I leave you now to a place far above;
my last words to you are that of LOVE.

MICHELLE PETERSEN 2012

Heart Strings Of Attachment . . . .

We are all connected in the web of life;
Soul brothers and soul sisters that may cross your path,
during the destiny of mankind's life.
The heart strings between us are attached at soul level;
They attach at the base of our life center's bevel.
That's why we feel each other's joy & sorrows as if it was our own;
When your sisters & brothers begin to stumble,
reach out your right hand;
for they may need your strong arm in order to stand!
Our words are important for they carry much weight;
Whether they are words that are good and uplifting,
or those which bring sorrow and feelings of hate.
Choose your actions and words with careful consideration;
For they attach at soul level and bring forth many revelations.
My hope is that these revelations will be;
From the Light & Love form our great Mother-Father's Spirit,
you see!

Plant the seeds of hope with your deeds of Loving Kindness;
Serve others with a humbled heart of respect,
And place our differences behind us.
Then this world will be a better place to live;
A heaven on earth.
Where people speak the highest gift that they possible can give.
This gift I speak of are words and deeds,
of the sweetest and deepest LOVE I believe.
The LOVE from your heart center is like the light of a candle;
May it always be lighted with Love from God's heart.

MICHELLE PETERSEN 2012.

Edwards Brothers Malloy
Oxnard, CA USA
August 4, 2014